Foreword

The study of minimum paths on or around polyhedra in Euclidean 3-space is of growing importance in robotics. This work presents new algorithms based on extensions of the Voronoi diagram. Since experience with new algorithms is also important, this work also describes a workbench to allow experimentation.

This book is based on the Ph.D. research of my former student, Varol Akman, who graduated from the Electrical, Computer, and Systems Engineering Dept. of Rensselaer Polytechnic Institute in August 1985.

We wish to thank the other members of his committee: Frank DiCesare, Mukkai S. Krishnamoorthy, and James M. Tien. We also wish to thank Herbert Freeman for employing him in the Image Processing Lab at RPI, Michael J. Wozny for employing him in the Center for Interactive Computer Graphics, and Edwin Rogers for granting free access to the Computer Science Dept. facilities.

This research has been supported by the National Science Foundation under grants ECS 80-21504 and ECS 83-51942, by the Schlumberger-Doll Research Center, Ridgefield, Connecticut, USA, by a Fulbright Award, and by the Middle East Technical University, Ankara, Turkey. The views expressed in this work are those of the author alone, and no endorsement is expressed or implied by the support.

Wm. Randolph Franklin
Rensselaer Polytechnic Institute
June 1986

Dedicated to my parents and my brother

For me there is only the traveling on paths that have heart, on any path that may have heart. There I travel, and the only worthwhile challenge is to traverse its full length. And there I travel, looking, looking, breathlessly.
- DON JUAN

Namely, because the shape of the whole universe is most perfect and, in fact, designed by the wisest creator, nothing in all of the world will occur in which no maximum or minimum rule is somehow shining forth.
- LEONHARD EULER

Whenever the local endpoint of the unknown quantity describes a straight line or a circle, a plane locus results, and when it describes a parabola, hyperbola, or ellipse, a solid locus results.
- PIERRE DE FERMAT

Is the three-dimensional shortest path problem NP-complete? For one, it does not seem to be in NP at all, because of the difficulty with the skew lines mentioned before. The difficulty is reminiscent of a similar one with the Euclidean traveling salesman problem and the precision required in evaluating tours, although the present situation is far more complex, and furthermore, there is no obvious discretization to help avoid the issue.
- CHRISTOS PAPADIMITRIOU

Table of Contents

1. Introduction

This introductory chapter has six sections. Section 1.1 is an overview of this text. In section 1.2 we give some prerequisite material and summarize our notation. In section 1.3 we define the problem that is central to the text. Section 1.4 describes the motivation for solving this problem. Section 1.5 recounts the relevant work by other researchers and section 1.6 outlines the remaining chapters of the text.

1.1. Overview

In this text, algebraic and geometric algorithms are presented to solve the general and some specific instances of the following problem which is (a variant of a problem) known as FINDPATH in artificial intelligence and robotics:

> Given a set of polyhedra and two external points (source and goal), calculate the shortest path between these points under the Euclidean metric, constrained to avoid intersections with the interiors of the given polyhedra. (In artificial intelligence, the shortness is not implied and rarely is this requirement of immediate interest.)

The shortest path is a polygonal path connecting the source and the goal, possibly bending at some edges of the given polyhedra while generally subtending equal entry and exit angles. The general problem can then be solved exactly using symbolic algebra and is based upon finding the real roots of a system of nonlinear equations stating the angular equality conditions, by classical elimination theory.

If approximate solutions are acceptable this can also be done using numerical methods such as Garcia and Zangwill's [1979, 1981] "continuation" framework, or using optimization methods to minimize a sum of square roots expressing the length of the shortest path. It is shown that Monte-Carlo algorithms such as [Metropolis et al 1953] are also useful in this regard.

In addition, two special cases are solved in this text where there exists a convex polyhedron, and the source and the goal are on its boundary or exterior. These solutions make use of the planar developments of polyhedra and polyhedral visibility.

Two Voronoi-based locus methods are also introduced to solve FINDPATH. These methods use preprocessing to speed up the subsequent searches for a shortest path. The first method partitions the boundary of a convex polyhedron given only the source on it so that, for a later goal point on the boundary, the shortest path is found efficiently. It makes use of standard point-location algorithms for a straight-edge planar subdivision once the partitioning is done. The second method, currently more of a descriptive nature than algorithmic, is based on Franklin's [1982] plane partitioning technique, and for a given source, divides the free space around polyhedra into regions bounded by high-order surfaces so that the shortest paths for all goals in a given region follow the same sequence of edges of the given polyhedra. This method makes use of a recent spatial point-location algorithm for arbitrary algebraic varieties due to Chazelle [1984].

Finally, guidelines are presented to build a "Geometer's Workbench" which would let one investigate shortest paths or other computational geometry problems of similar nature. These guidelines are then placed into a concrete context by reviewing a prototype called SP which implements some of the above algorithms and allows experimentation with shortest paths. Open problems and suggested research topics conclude the text.

While this monograph is largely based upon my RPI dissertation [Akman 1985], it is a major rewriting and incorporates all the important developments that have taken place since then. The style is also more expository and a good deal of material regarding SP has been left out since it would convey little information for the general reader.

Part of the contents of this text previously appeared as individual papers. The reader is referred to [Akman 1983], [Franklin and Akman 1984], [Franklin and Akman July 1985], [Franklin et al 1985], [Franklin and Akman June 1985], [Franklin and Akman 1986], and [Franklin and Akman 1985] for further details.

1.2. Prerequisites and Notation

For classical material on polyhedra, graphs, and algebra, we follow Grunbaum [1967], Harary [1972], and van der Waerden [1977]. A standard reference on computational geometry is the recent text of Preparata and Shamos [1985]; Sedgewick [1983], Shamos [1978], Mehlorn [1984], and Lee and Preparata [1984] are also useful sources. For concrete complexity we follow Garey and Johnson [1979].

In general, explanations of the terms and the concepts left undefined in this text can be found in the above references and will not be given here. This is not expected to be a potential nuisance for the reader since we shall need only the most elementary notions in the above-mentioned sources.

With few exceptions, we shall be concerned with R^3, the three-dimensional real Euclidean space, or 3-space in short. Points of R^3, as well as the corresponding vectors, will be denoted by lower case letters. By $d(a,b)$ we shall denote the Euclidean distance between the points a and b whereas $d(a)$ will denote the length of vector a. The number of elements in set A is shown as $\text{card}A$. The scalar product of vectors $a,b\,\varepsilon R^3$ is denoted by $<a,b>$ while $a\times b$ is their vector product. The affine hull of set A is denoted by $\text{aff}A$ whereas $\text{conv}A$ is its convex hull. The interior, boundary, and exterior of a set A are respectively $\text{int}A$, $\text{bd}A$, and $\text{cl}A$. For a polyhedral set A, the totality of the extreme points of A is the vertices of A and is shown as $\text{vert}A$; 1-faces of A are called the edges of A and are denoted by $\text{edge}A$. Maximal proper faces are the facets of A and their union is equal to $\text{bd}A$. (Departing from Grunbaum's terminology, we shall use from now on the more widespread term "face" instead of "facet.") To prevent potential confusions, we shall use the terms vertex, edge, and path *exclusively* for polygons and polyhedra. For graphs, we shall use the less common terms node, arc, and walk, respectively.

To estimate bounds, the standard notation (reviewed below to overcome the slight nuances in the literature) will be used. Briefly, let $f(n)$ and $g(n)$ be functions of integer $n \geq 0$. Then $f(n)=O(g(n))$ implies that there exists c and n_0 such that $|f(n)|<cg(n)$ for $n>n_0$. On the other hand, $f(n)=o(g(n))$ implies that $\lim_{n\to\infty} f(n)/g(n)=0$. Finally, $f(n)=\Theta(g(n))$ implies that there exists c_1 and c_2 (where $c_1 c_2>0$), and n_0 such that $c_1 g(n)<f(n)<c_2 g(n)$ for $n>n_0$; $f(n)=\Omega(g(n))$ implies that $g(n)=O(f(n))$.

1.3. FINDPATH - Problem Statement

Let $\{P_1,P_2,\cdots,P_n\}$ be a prescribed set of disjoint polyhedra and $s,g\,\varepsilon R^3$ be distinct points which are not internal to any P_i. The class of rectifiable curves which have endpoints s and g and which do not intersect any $\text{int}P_i$ will be denoted by $C(s,g;P)$. For C in this class, $l(C)$ will denote the length of C under the Euclidean (L_2) metric. An interesting problem in computational geometry (historically, with roots in artificial intelligence) asks for the shortest among these curves and will be the subject of this text:

FINDPATH

INSTANCE: Polyhedra $P = \{P_1, P_2, \cdots, P_n\}$ such that $P_i \cap P_j = \phi$, $i \neq j$, and $s, g \in R^3$ such that $s \neq g$ and s, g do not belong to intP_i, $1 \leq i \leq n$.

QUESTION: Which $C \in C(s, g; P)$ has the shortest Euclidean length?

The above version of FINDPATH is an *optimization* problem and in the sequel, when we refer to FINDPATH without any qualification we shall mean FINDPATH (optimization). The following defines the *decision* version of FINDPATH:

FINDPATH (decision)

INSTANCE: Same as in FINDPATH and additionally, a positive integer k.

QUESTION: Is there a $C \in C(s, g; P)$ such that $l(C) \leq k$?

We shall return to the interplay between these two versions of FINDPATH after the following theorem which must be intuitively clear:

THEOREM 1.1. There exists a $\overline{C} \in C(s, g; P)$ such that for all $C \in C(s, g; P)$, $l(\overline{C}) \leq l(C)$. Moreover, every such $\overline{C}$ is a polygonal path with its possible bend points belonging to some edges of some members of P.

Proof. Our proof will follow a similar theorem of Chein and Steinberg [1983] in 2-space. Let C be any curve in $C(s, g; P)$. If any part of C lies outside $H = \text{conv}P'$ where $P' = \{s, g\} \cup (\bigcup_{1}^{n} \text{vert}P_i)$, then let x be the first point at which C leaves H and let y_1 be the point at which C first returns. Let F be the face on bd$H$ which contains y_1 and let y be the last point where C enters H on F. Then $C = C_1 C_2 C_3 C_4$ where C_1, C_2, C_3, and C_4 are respectively curves from s to x, from x to y_1, from y_1 to y, and from y to g; with C_1 lying inside H, C_2 lying outside H, and C_4 starting at int$H$ (figure 1.1). Let C'_2 be the shorter polygonal path on bd$H$ between x and y_1, C'_3 be the line segment $y_1 y$, and let $C' = C_1 C'_2 C'_3 C_4$. (Here the segment $y_1 y$ is meaningful since F is convex.) Then $l(C'_3) \leq l(C_3)$ and by the convexity of H, one has $l(C'_2) \leq l(C_2)$; so $l(C') \leq l(C)$. Furthermore C' does not intersect the members of P and thus belongs to $C(s, g; P)$. We shall therefore restrict our attention to curves C lying entirely within H.

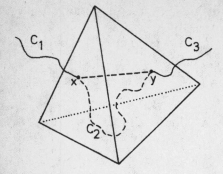

Figure 1.2 A curve intersecting the 3-simplex of theorem 1.1.

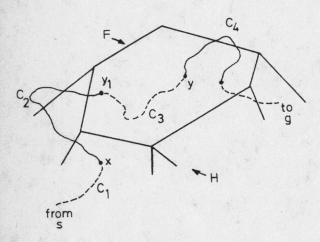

Figure 1.1 Curves C_1, C_2, C_3, and C_4 of theorem 1.1.

Decompose $H - (\bigcup_1^n P_i)$ into 3-simplexes in such a way that any pair of sim-
plexes either have no common points or share a face (of arbitrary dimension). If
C, lying within H, first enters the interior of a 3-simplex of this decomposition
at x and leaves it for the last time at y, then $C = C_1 C_2 C_3$ where C_2 is a curve
from x to y. Letting $C'_2 = xy$ and setting $C' = C_1 C'_2 C_3$, we have $l(C') \leq l(C)$.
Clearly, $C' \varepsilon C(s, g; P)$ since if C' cuts a face of this 3-simplex, so does C
(figure 1.2).

Now we can further restrict our attention to polygonal paths within H. Suppose $C = b_1 b_2 \cdots b_t$ is such a path with bend points b_i where for convenience,
$b_1 = s$ and $b_t = g$. If there is a bend point of C not belonging to an edge of some
polyhedron in P, then let b_i, $1 < i < t$, be the first such point. Consider the intersections of all polyhedra in P with the triangle $T = b_{i-1} b_i b_{i+1}$. The intersections
make up a set of polygons (possibly degenerated to line segments or points) in
aff$T$. Let V denote the totality of the vertices of these polygons and consider
$H_i = \text{conv}(\{b_{i-1} b_{i+1}\} \cup V)$. If V is empty then let $C'_2 = b_{i-1} b_{i+1}$; otherwise
bdH_i consists of $b_{i-1} b_{i+1}$ and another polygonal path C'_2 where
$l(C'_2) \leq l(b_{i-1} b_i b_{i+1})$ by convexity. Accordingly, $l(C') \leq l(C)$ if $C' = C_1 C'_2 C_3$ and
C' also belongs to $C(s, g; P)$ (figure 1.3). Continuing likewise, we can reduce
the number of bend points of C which are not on the edges of any P_i one by
one, while simultaneously shortening $l(C)$, until we obtain the required polygonal path $\overline{C}$. $\square$

It is noted that the polygonal path $\overline{C}$ found in theorem 1.1 is not necessarily
unique. We shall call any such path an s-to-g *shortest path*. Thus, FINDPATH
asks for the characterization (i.e. the determination of the bend points) of one s-
to-g shortest path. The following shows that listing all such paths will in general
require exponential time in card$P$:

THEOREM 1.2. There exists instances of FINDPATH where there are
$\Theta(2^n)$ s-to-g shortest paths.

Proof. We shall demonstrate this with an example workspace in 2-space
(figure 1.4). It is then easy to extend this example to 3-space by erecting prisms
for each polygon. In figure 1.4 we require that $n \geq 4$ and even, and all odd-
numbered polygons are large enough so that a shortest path cannot tour around
them. We also require that all even-numbered polygons are squares whose
centers of mass are on line segment sg; similarly, the nonreflex vertices of P_1

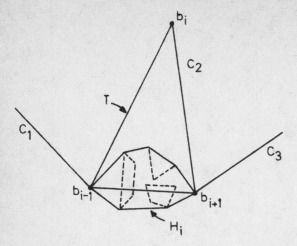

Figure 1.3 The intersections of P_i with the triangle $b_{i-1} b_i\ b_{i+1}$ of theorem 1.1 shown with dashed lines.

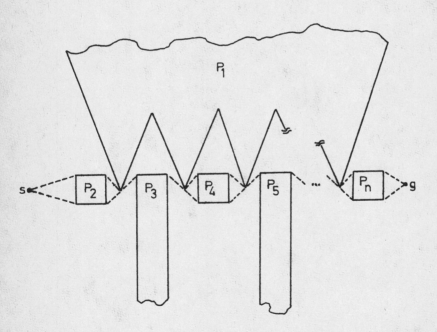

Figure 1.4 The workspace of theorem 1.2 which gives rise to $2^{n/2}$ s-to-g shortest paths.

are aligned on sg. It is seen that for the described workspace there are exactly $2^{n/2}$ s-to-g shortest paths. $\square$

Now we return to the relationship between FINDPATH and FINDPATH (decision). It may be thought that each of the optimization, *evaluation* (i.e. the one that asks only the length of the shortest path), and decision versions of FINDPATH, in this order, is not harder than the preceding one. That is, if we are given the bend points of a shortest path then we can compute its length, and certainly compare this number with an integer. However the cost of performing the latter operation deserves close attention. Consider the following problem which we shall call:

FINDPATH (suboptimality)

INSTANCE: Same as in FINDPATH and additionally, an s-to-g polygonal path C which is free of intersections with the given polyhedra, i.e. $C \varepsilon C(s,g;P)$.

QUESTION: Is C suboptimal, i.e. Is there a second obstacle-avoiding s-to-g polygonal path $C' \varepsilon C(s,g;P)$ where $l(C') \leq l(C)$?

Clearly, FINDPATH (suboptimality) requires a way to compare the lengths of two paths, $l(C)$ and $l(C')$, which are basically sums of square roots.

Although it is known that a number such as $m^{1/n}$ is irrational in general, it is nontrivial to extend such a result to linear combinations of radicals, e.g. the sum $13^{1/4}+4^{1/7}+79^{1/18}$. The crucial question is: Is such a sum irrational whenever its terms do not obviously cancel out? An affirmative answer to this question was given by Besicovitch in 1940; we shall offer an equivalent formulation of his theorem:

THEOREM 1.3. Let $\{e_i\}$ denote the set of n^k radicals

$$(p_1^{m(1)}p_2^{m(2)} \cdots p_k^{m(k)})^{1/n}$$

where $0 \leq m(i) < n$, $1 \leq i \leq k$. Then the set $\{e_i\}$ is linearly independent over the rationals, Q.

Proof. cf. Richards [1974]. (The proof for square roots, $n=2$, is easier.) $\square$

The application of theorem 1.3 to our case can then be stated as follows: If $p_1, p_2, \cdots, p_n$ are positive integers, coprime in pairs and each p_i not a perfect square, then the 2^n algebraic integers $(p_1^{m(1)}p_2^{m(2)} \cdots p_n^{m(n)})^{1/2}$, where $m(i)$ is either 0 or 1, are linearly independent over Q. Thus, an expression such as

$7\sqrt{19}+3\sqrt{117}+9\sqrt{6}$ is irrational, meaning that in comparing such an expression against an integer we are not worried about the "equality" case since that would never arise (after establishing the coprime- and nonperfect squareness).

But we still have decide about the "less than" case. Returning to the comparison of two lengths above, the obvious method of repeated squaring to eliminate the square roots has an exponential worst-case complexity. In fact, there is no *known* method to guarantee the correctness of this comparison with only a polynomial effort in the number of square roots, r, involved. Garey at al [1976] cite the best known bound on the number of places of accuracy as $O(m\,2^r)$ where m is the number of digits in the original symbolic expression. The reader is referred to Akman and Franklin [1986] for a review of this problem.

Mignotte [1982] considers the following related problem. If a and b are given algebraic numbers and if we know the approximations a' and b' for them (computed numerically), can we decide whether $a=b$? That is, is there a "numerical" proof of $a=b$ in contrast to an algebraic proof which is difficult in many cases? He proves that this is indeed possible showing that a numerical attack is feasible to simplify radicals.

In view of the above discussion, one may be tempted to think that problems such as FINDPATH (or GEOMETRIC TRAVELING SALESMAN [Garey et al 1976]) are intractable simply because of the evaluation issues stemming from the irrational square roots (surds). However, Papadimitriou [1977] shows that this is not really so, at least for the GEOMETRIC TRAVELING SALESMAN problem. He defines a new distance metric $d'(x,y)=\text{ceil}(d(x,y))$ and proves that the problem remains NP-complete even under this metric.

1.4. Motivation

The history of mathematics is full of reinventions. In that respect, the shortest path problem is no exception. It is common knowledge that problems of this sort are treated under the general title of the *calculus of variations,* an area of mathematics that deals with optimal forms in geometry and nature, and problems of maxima and minima. The calculus of variations traditionally considered only curved objects and is thus hardly useful for FINDPATH (with polyhedral objects). We shall take a short look at the history of the subject which is nevertheless illuminating.

The Greeks knew that the shortest path between two points in the plane is always a straight line. On a curved surface, however, there are in general no straight lines. Thus it is not at all obvious what the shortest path would be on a complicated surface. (Hildebrant and Tromba [1985] offer a detailed history of this subject.) Finding the shortest connection between two points on a cylinder or cone is easy. The idea is to spread the object under investigation out onto the plane without distortion. On the other hand, one can show that no part of a sphere can be mapped without distortion onto a plane. The proof makes use of the *Gaussian curvature* of a surface which measures how curved a surface is at any point. The 1827 *theorema egregium* (remarkable theorem) of Gauss treats this problem and explains why one cannot make perfect maps of the surface of our planet.

The first paper on the shortest line between two points on a general surface is Euler's *De linea brevissima in superficie quacunque duo quaelibet puncta jungente* (On the shortest line on an arbitrary surface connecting any two points whatsoever), published in 1732. Here Euler gives the popular "string" analogy to solve the problem: Fix a string at one of the points and pull it taut in the direction of the other. Seeing the method fail for a concave surface Euler also developed a technique based on differential calculus and a theorem of Johann Bernoulli which reads:

> At each point of a shortest line, the corresponding osculating plane of the line intersects the tangent plane to the surface at that point in a right angle.

Stated succinctly, Bernoulli's theorem becomes: Curves of shortest length must be portions of geodesics.

The study of geodesics caused interesting competition among the leading mathematicians of the 17th and 18th centuries, including Newton, Leibniz, Johann and Jakob Bernoulli brothers, Marquis de l'Hospital, Euler, and Pascal. For example, in [Hildebrant and Tromba 1985] it is told that:

> Johann Bernoulli, in August 1697, publicly posed the problem of finding the shortest line between two given points on a convex surface. This was meant as a challenge to his brother Jakob, with whom he was publicly feuding. The unfortunate rivalry of the two brothers eventually became so intense, and their polemics so ugly, that the scientific journals of the time declined to publish them.

Like many other problems in computational geometry (GEOMETRIC TRAVELING SALESMAN being a prime example) FINDPATH can be described in simple terms even to a novice whereas its solution seems to involve many difficult problems. Alexandrov [1958], Courant and Robbins [1941], Efimov [1962], and Lyusternik [1964] study some relevant problems such as the planar developments of polyhedra but their arguments are frequently informal and non-constructive. Saaty [1970] defines a specific instance of FINDPATH that we shall call BOUNDARY FINDPATH (cf. section 3.1) and hints at the usefulness of planar developments to solve it but does not attempt to formulate a solution. Jacobson and Yocom [June 1966, October 1966] deal with interesting problems in the proximity of FINDPATH such as shortest paths within polygons or cubes; yet their approach is far from being algorithmic.

To summarize, while TRAVELING SALESMAN has received wide attention for a long time, it seems that FINDPATH has essentially been overlooked from an algorithmic viewpoint until the last couple of years.

The recent creation of interest in FINDPATH owes to the advent of *task-level (model-based)* robot programming systems such as the SHRDLU program of Winograd [Winston 1977]. Although SHRDLU was essentially built to study natural language understanding, its geometric nature makes it a good candidate to demonstrate our point. (The reader is referred to [Moravec 1980] and [Rowat 1979] for recent systems which may essentially be regarded as model-based.) SHRDLU simulates a robot manipulator working in a *blocks world*, a workspace solely cluttered with simple objects such as cubes, pyramids, boxes, and so on. Users requesting a particular action state it in simple English. Thus, requests such as "Pick up a red block," or "Stack up both of the red blocks and either a green cube or a pyramid" call for goals to be achieved by SHRDLU. A geometric path planner designs and submits these plans to a manipulator controller which eventually simulates them. During the design phase, the path planner of SHRDLU utilizes a geometric model of the workspace.

The path planner comprises three important functions. The function FINDSPACE tries to find a place for a given block so that the block will be stable on its new support. If FINDSPACE cannot determine a suitable space, MAKESPACE intervenes to clear away some obstacles. Finally, FINDPATH moves a block to a specified location while avoiding clashes with the other blocks. It is possible to reduce (albeit by introducing complications) an "object" FINDPATH problem of this sort to a "point" FINDPATH problem, i.e. the version we shall study in this text. Lozano-Perez [1981, 1983] cites an approach which is known as the *configuration space (Cspace)* method for the reduction. In simple terms, the *Cspace* method maps an object movement problem to a point movement problem by simultaneously growing the obstacles in the workspace and by shrinking the object to be moved to a *reference point* [Lozano-Perez and Wesley 1979]. This method gives exact results for movements consisting of only translations. Rotations make the method much difficult to implement since now one has to deal with higher-order surfaces with trigonometric equations but an approximation scheme which allows rotations is still possible [Brooks and Lozano-Perez 1982].

1.5. Related Research on Motion Planning

Directly relevant work on 3-dimensional FINDPATH is quite recent. We shall review works by Sharir and Schorr [1986], O'Rourke et al [1985], Papadimitriou [1985], Mitchell and Papadimitriou [1985], Reif and Storer [1985], and others in more detail in section 4.3. On the other hand, there is a wealth of material on 2-dimensional FINDPATH and in the general area of what we shall call *motion planning*. We shall somewhat artificially divide this material into three classes and review only the important representatives in each class.

1.5.1. More Practical Works

Howden [1968] presents a simple program which determines in discrete 2-space if a sofa can be moved from a source to a goal point inside a house. He calls this the SOFA PROBLEM. Other early papers on the SOFA PROBLEM include those by Moser [1966], Sebastian [1970], Goldberg [1969], and Maruyama [1973]. Wangdahl et al [1974] look at the SOFA PROBLEM from the viewpoint of minimum-trajectory pipe routing as faced e.g. in ship design.

Eastman [1970] defines the representational and data structural requirements for space planning problems like the SOFA PROBLEM. Boyse [1979] considers the problem of interference detection among polyhedral objects. He discusses two types of interference checking: (i) Detection of intersections among stationary objects, and (ii) Detection of collisions among moving objects. The check in (i) is crucial in a preliminary phase of FINDPATH where the disjointness of the given obstacles must be guaranteed. Recently, Canny [1986] obtained interesting results on the problem of collision detection for moving polyhedra (also see section 4.3).

Udupa [1977], in a pioneering work on the computational aspects of robotics, maintains the free space as a variable resolution description of the feasible positions of the reference point found via the *Cspace* method. Safe paths are then found by recursively introducing new goals into a linear path until the complete path is confined to the free space. Sussman [1975] works on heuristics for solving FINDSPACE; his work is oriented toward artificial intelligence and is in the spirit of Winograd's.

Lozano-Perez and Wesley [1979] present an algorithm for 2-dimensional FINDPATH where there are polygonal obstacles with forbidden interiors. Their algorithm uses the fact that the shortest path is a polygonal path whose bend points are some vertices of the given polygons. It first constructs a *visibility graph (Vgraph)* whose nodes consist of $\{s,g\} \cup (\bigcup_{1}^{n} \text{vert}P_i)$ where P_i's are the given polygons. An arc in the *Vgraph* connects a pair of nodes corresponding to a pair of vertices visible to each other and carries a weight equal to the Euclidean distance between these vertices. It is easy to search a *Vgraph* using a shortest path algorithm for graphs (cf. Tarjan [1983]) once it is available. Lee and Preparata [1984] mention a result of Lee [1978] showing that 2-dimensional FINDPATH with arbitrarily oriented disjoint line segments as obstacles is solvable in $O(m^2 \log m)$ time where m is the total number of segments. Special configurations of the segments make more efficient techniques available. Tompa [1981] gives several $O(m)$ algorithms for the case of presorted vertical rays each extending either to $+\infty$ or $-\infty$. Sharir and Schorr [1986] also have an $O(m \log m)$ algorithm if the obstructions are all vertical lines with several point apertures. Since a *Vgraph* on m nodes where $m = \sum_{1}^{n} \text{card}(\text{vert}P_i)$ has in general $\Omega(m^2)$ arcs, Lozano-Perez and Wesley's graph search has an $\Omega(m^2)$ lower bound even assuming the *Vgraph* available at the outset. Lee and Preparata [1984], in their quest for an $o(m^2)$ time algorithm, propose two improvements. They show that there are $O(m \log m)$ solutions: (i) When the given segments form a simple polygon to which the source and the goal are internal, and (ii) When the given segments are disjoint and at the same time parallel to each other.

The best algorithm to solve the general instance of FINDPATH in 2-space is due to Ta. Asano et al [1986] and independently due to Welzl [1985]. Both algorithms run in time $O(m^2)$; however it is currently an interesting question whether this is a strict lower bound since it may after all be possible to store the information implicit in a *Vgraph* in space $o(m^2)$.

Rohnert [1985] studies the shortest path problem in 2-space for exclusively convex workspaces. Assuming that there are f disjoint obstacles with a total of m vertices, he can compute the shortest path between arbitrary query points in time $O(f^2+m\log m)$, after a preprocessing cost of $O(m+f^2\log m)$ and using space of $O(m+f^2)$. He [Rohnert 1986] then improves this to time $O(m\log m+f^2\log m)$ using only $O(m)$ space. The latter paper also considers the case of f polygons that may intersect pairwise at most twice. In this case, Rohnert's contribution is an algorithm with query time $O(m\log m+f^2)$, after investing $O(m\log m+f^3)$ preprocessing time and $O(m+f^2)$ space.

A polygon in R^2 that can translate and rotate has three degrees of freedom whose legal values are constrained by the other obstacles in the workspace. Lozano-Perez [1983] considers these degrees of freedom to be the three Cartesian coordinates of a point that must move while avoiding obstacles in R^3 and then uses an approximate 3-dimensional FINDPATH algorithm. His student Nguyen [1984] gives a heuristic algorithm for 2-dimensional FINDPATH. His algorithm is based on describing the free space as a network of "linked cones." In a way, cones capture the freeways and the bottlenecks between obstacles while the links capture the connectivity of the free space. In an earlier work, Brooks [1983] represents the free space as a union of overlapping cones and gives an algorithm which finds "good" paths for convex polygonal bodies. The paths are good in the sense that the distance of closest approach to an obstacle over a computed path is far from the minimal over the class of paths homotopic to it. Thus, a real robot following this path will be securer. Brooks and Lozano-Perez [1982] describe an implementation of 2-dimensional FINDPATH with rotations allowed. Donald [June 1983] presents a technique for hypothesizing a "channel volume" through the free space containing a class of collision-free paths. His channel volume starts out by surrounding the moving object at the source and grows toward the goal point.

Although they use the L_1 (Manhattan or rectilinear) metric, several other algorithms for 2-dimensional FINDPATH are also important. Larson and Li [1981] give a Dijkstra-type algorithm for finding the minimum length path between the source and the goal in the presence of polygonal barriers. Lipski [1983] deals with m horizontal and vertical line segments in the plane. He gives an $O(m\log^2 m)$ time algorithm (which can be improved to $O(m\log m\log\log m)$ using more complicated data structures) to find, for a given source segment, the shortest paths to all other goal segments. Wong [1979] and Mitchell [1986] also employ L_1 metric to compute shortest paths on a plane with barriers. Rezende et al [1985] show that there has to be a path of minimum length between two given points (in the presence of rectangular barriers) which is monotone in at least one of x or y directions. They then present an $O(m\log m)$ time algorithm for m rectangles. In the locus version of their solution a shortest path is reported in time $O(k+\log m)$ (after $O(m\log m)$ preprocessing) for a path with k bend points.

1.5.2. Complexity-Theoretic Works

Donald [August 1983] gives a fine tutorial on the geometric complexity of motion. Reif [1979], in a pioneering paper on the complexity of motion planning, treats the MOVER'S PROBLEM, another name for the SOFA PROBLEM. He approximates the sofa and the house as systems of linear inequalities which are slightly perturbed by a small amount ε. His algorithm gives an indeterminate answer only if the sofa, shrunk by a factor $1-\varepsilon$, can be moved from the source to the goal but when grown by a factor of $1+\varepsilon$ the move is impossible. He then extends the problem to allow a sofa to consist of multiple polygons linked together at several vertices and proves that this instance is PSPACE-hard.

In a series of seminal papers, Schwartz and his students study the complexity of the PIANO MOVER'S PROBLEM, yet another name for the SOFA PROBLEM. In the first paper of the series, Schwartz and Sharir [1983, part I] give a topological analysis of the space of positions of a polygon moving in the plane in the presence of polygonal obstacles. In the second paper [Schwartz and Sharir 1983, part II] they work with the manifold of allowable positions of a manipulator and reduce the motion planning problem to the problem of finding the connected components of an algebraic manifold. They partition this manifold into connected subregions of simple structure which they call "cells." Their techniques makes use of Tarski's [1951] decision method for elementary algebra and geometry, and its more efficient refinements introduced by Collins and his coworkers [Arnon et al 1984, parts I and II]. Schwartz and Sharir's algorithm is polynomial in the number of edges of the obstacles but exponential in the degrees of freedom. Schwartz and Sharir [Fall 1983, part III] solve the following restricted instance of the SOFA PROBLEM: Given several 2-dimensional discs inside a polygon, find a continuous motion connecting two specified configurations of these objects during which they avoid collision with the polygonal edges and with each other. Their algorithm is polynomial in the number of edges of the polygon but again exponential in the number of moving discs. This is an expected result since Spirakis and Yap [1984] proved the strong NP-hardness of moving many discs. Sharir and Ariel-Sheffi [1984, part IV] treat the case of a "spider" with several arms. This is a 2-dimensional robot consisting of several arms all joined at one common endpoint and free to rotate past each other. Schwartz and Sharir [1984, part V] solve the motion planning problem for a line segment moving amidst polyhedra. A paper by O'Dunlaing et al [1983] describes other approaches to motion planning using notions such as "retraction" which has interesting connections with differential topology.

Kedem and Sharir [1985] give an $O(m \log^2 m)$ algorithm for the following specific instance of MOVER'S PROBLEM: Given a convex polygon with a constant number of vertices and a set of convex obstacles with a total of m vertices, determine whether there is an obstacle-avoiding and purely translational motion for the given polygon.

Hopcroft and his associates also worked on several motion planning problems. (A recent survey by Hopcroft [1986] summarizes some results.) Specifically, Hopcroft et al [August 1984] investigate the 2-dimensional SOFA PROBLEM in which the object is a manipulator with an arbitrary number of joints. They give two polynomial algorithms: one for moving the manipulator confined within a circle from a given configuration to another, and the other for moving it from its initial position to a position in which its tip reaches to a given point inside the circle. In closely related works [Hopcroft et al 1982, 1985] they prove that a planar linkage can be constrained to stay inside a bounded region with a straight-edge boundary by only adding a polynomial number of new links to it. They also show that the question of whether a planar linkage in some initial configuration can be moved so that a designated joint of it reaches to a given point in the plane is PSPACE-hard (also see [Joseph and Plantinga 1985]).

Recently, Kantabutra and Kosaraju [1986] presented an algorithm with $O(n)$ computation time to move an n-link arm confined in a circular region to any reachable configuration in $O(n)$ moves. They also gave algorithms to compute the regions reachable by the joints of such an arm in time $O(n)$ and to plan the motion so as to involve the minimum number of moves in the obstacle-free plane in time $O(n^3)$.

Hopcroft and Wilfong [1986] deal with the motion of objects in contact. In another paper [Hopcroft and Wilfong 1984], they study the motion planning issues for multiple objects where each object is a polygon with edges parallel to the axes of R^2. They show that for a rectangular workspace this problem is in PSPACE. Since Hopcroft et al [Winter 1984] proved that this problem (which they named the WAREHOUSEMAN'S PROBLEM) is PSPACE-hard, the problem is clearly PSPACE-complete.

Reif and Sharir [1985] investigate the computational complexity of planning the motion of a body in order to avoid collision with "asteroids" of known, readily computable trajectories. They provide evidence that the 3-dimensional problem is intractable even if the "spaceship" has only a constant number of degrees of freedom. Specifically, the problem is proven to be PSPACE-hard if the spaceship has a velocity modulus bound and NP-hard if no such bound is imposed. In both cases the spaceship has six degrees of freedom.

1.5.3. Voronoi-Based Works

A detailed review of Voronoi diagrams is beyond the limits of this monograph. Section 4.1 summarizes some essential material and points out to major references.

O'Dunlaing and Yap [1985] use the Voronoi method for planning the motion of a disc in a 2-dimensional region bounded by polygonal obstacles. They construct a Voronoi diagram using the obstacles. The diagram is a planar graph of straight and parabolic edges and is characterized as a set of points which are equidistant from at least two obstacles. Kirkpatrick [1979] gives an $O(m \log m)$ time algorithm for this problem where m is the total number of edges of the obstacles; a somewhat simpler but $O(m \log^2 m)$ time algorithm is presented by Lee and Drysdale [1981]. If there is a continuous collision-free motion of the disc between the source and the goal positions of its center, then O'Dunlaing and Yap [1985] show that there is another motion of the same sort during which the center of the disc moves entirely along the Voronoi diagram. (Chew [1985] proved that the *shortest* path for such a disc can be computed in time $O(m^2 \log m)$.) In a descendant of this work, O'Dunlaing et al [November 1984, parts I and II] tackle the case of a moving line segment ("ladder") instead of a disc. They present an algorithm running in time $O(m^2 \log m \log^* m)$ for constructing a skeleton representation of a generalized Voronoi diagram. Theirs is a variant of Kirkpatrick's [1979] continuous skeletons. Recently, Leven and Sharir [1985] slightly improved O'Dunlaing et al's time bound to $O(m^2 \log m)$.

1.6. Organization

After this introductory chapter, the remaining parts are structured as follows. Chapter 2 discusses the general solution of FINDPATH and several ways of speeding it up. Chapter 3 deals with two special instances of FINDPATH, both in the presence of a single convex obstacle. Chapter 4 offers two Voronoi-based locus approaches to solve FINDPATH more efficiently after some preprocessing. Chapter 5 describes the functionalities expected from a "Geometer's Workbench" which lets one study geometric problems of the sort treated here. It then exemplifies these ideas using SP, a system written to explore and to experiment with shortest path algorithms. Finally, chapter 6 cites important open problems along with conclusions.

2. Solution of the General Instance of FINDPATH

This chapter has two sections. In section 2.1 we study FINDPATH in its full generality and give a simple yet very inefficient algorithm. Section 2.2 offers some methods to speed this algorithm up. Unfortunately, a polynomial-time algorithm for the general case is highly unexpected and it is commonly believed that the problem is NP-hard.

2.1. A Brute-Force Algorithm

In this section we shall give an algorithm which, although very inefficiently, is able to solve FINDPATH. Throughout this book, we shall assume, without loss of generality, that line segment sg itself is *not* the shortest path. This can be checked by applying standard line-polyhedron intersection detection algorithms.

We shall first solve the following problem which will be the main ingredient of our algorithm for FINDPATH:

OPTIMAL LINE VISIT

INSTANCE: Lines $L = \{L_1, L_2, \cdots, L_n\}$ and points s, g, all situated in R^3. (Each line is specified by a pair of distinct points.)

QUESTION: What is the s-to-g shortest path constrained to pass through the sequence of lines $L_1, L_2, \cdots, L_n$ in that order?

It is clear that the shortest path is a polygonal path in this case too. Let $b_1, b_2, \cdots, b_n$ denote the bend points of the shortest path on $L_1, L_2, \cdots, L_n$, respectively. For notational ease, we shall take $b_0 = s$ and $b_{n+1} = g$. The 3-dimensional unit vectors along each L_i will be denoted by u_i; their direction along their associated line can be arbitrary.

LEMMA 2.1. For $1 \leq i \leq n$, the angle between the vectors $b_{i-1}b_i$ and u_i is equal to the angle between the vectors $b_i b_{i+1}$ and u_i (figure 2.1).

Proof. This is well-known; Sharir and Schorr [1986] give a proof. □

LEMMA 2.2. The solution of OPTIMAL LINE VISIT is unique.

Proof. cf. Sharir and Schorr [1986]. □

With the aid of these lemmas, it is easy to formulate a solution for FINDPATH. From lemma 2.1, the bend points of the shortest path satisfy the

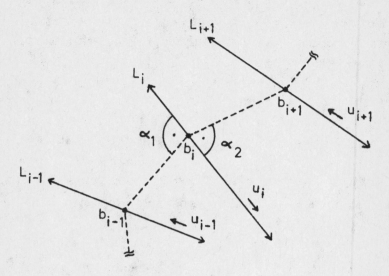

Figure 2.1 The angles α_1 and α_2 are equal if these bend points belong to a shortest path.

following vector equation for all $1 \leq i \leq n$:

$$<b_{i-1}b_i,u_i>/d(b_{i-1},b_i)=<b_ib_{i+1},u_i>/d(b_i,b_{i+1}) \tag{1}$$

Denoting the pair of points defining L_i by f_i and g_i, we also have the following vector equation for all $1 \leq i \leq n$:

$$b_i = f_i + x_i(g_i - f_i) \tag{2}$$

where x_i is L_i's parameter. Substituting the values of b_i found in (2) in (1) and using the fact that:

$$u_i = f_i g_i / d(f_i, g_i)$$

we obtain n nonlinear equations in n unknowns as follows:

$$Q_1(x_1, x_2) = 0$$

$$Q_2(x_1, x_2, x_3) = 0$$

$$\cdots$$

$$Q_i(x_{i-1}, x_i, x_{i+1}) = 0 \tag{3}$$

$$\cdots$$

$$Q_{n-1}(x_{n-2}, x_{n-1}, x_n) = 0$$

$$Q_n(x_{n-1}, x_n) = 0$$

In (3) we note three properties. First, each equation is a quartic (after removing the square roots caused by u_i's) in at most three variables. Second, the polynomials Q_i, $1 < i < n$ are dependent only on three unknowns, namely, x_{i-1}, x_i, x_{i+1}. Third, both Q_1 and Q_n have only two unknowns since b_0 and b_{n+1} are constant points.

Since we have n independent equations in n unknowns in (3), we can solve this system to determine the real root $(x_1, x_2, \cdots, x_n)$ using the classical theory of elimination (cf. van der Waerden [1977], Collins [1971], Lazard [1981] for a detailed description; Ku and Adler [1969] and Moses [1966] are good short expositions). Once the parameters x_i's are known, the bend points b_i's are easily computed using (2).

The idea of elimination is based on the polynomial resultants. We assume that the reader is familiar with the latter and omit several definitions and theorems. The crux of the elimination theory is the following:

THEOREM 2.1. Let F be an algebraically closed field. Let

$$A(x_1, x_2, \cdots, x_r) = \sum_0^m A_i(x_1, x_2, \cdots, x_{r-1}) x_r^i$$

$$B(x_1, x_2, \cdots, x_r) = \sum_0^n B_i(x_1, x_2, \cdots, x_{r-1}) x_r^i$$

be members of field $F[x_1, x_2, \cdots, x_r]$, of positive degrees m and n in x_r, and let $C(x_1, x_2, \cdots, x_{r-1})$ be the resultant of A and B with respect to x_r, the last unknown. (This will be denoted by $C = \text{res}(A, B)$ from now on.) If $(a_1, a_2, \cdots, a_r)$ is a common zero of A and B, then $C(a_1, a_2, \cdots, a_{r-1}) = 0$. Conversely, if $C(a_1, a_2, \cdots, a_{r-1}) = 0$, then at least one of the following conditions holds:

$$A_m(a_1, a_2, \cdots, a_{r-1}) = \cdots = A_0(a_1, a_2, \cdots, a_{r-1}) = 0$$

$$B_n(a_1, a_2, \cdots, a_{r-1}) = \cdots = B_0(a_1, a_2, \cdots, a_{r-1}) = 0$$

$$A_m(a_1, a_2, \cdots, a_{r-1}) = B_n(a_1, a_2, \cdots, a_{r-1}) = 0$$

For some $a_r \varepsilon F$ it is true that $A(a_1, a_2, \cdots, a_r) = B(a_1, a_2, \cdots, a_r) = 0$

Proof. cf. Collins [1971]. □

Theorem 2.1 suggests the following method to calculate the solution of a system of n polynomial equations in n unknowns. Let $A_i(x_1, x_2, \cdots, x_n) = 0$, $1 \leq i \leq n$, be the given system of equations. Now let:

$$B_i(x_1, x_2, \cdots, x_{n-1}) = \text{res}(A_i, A_n)$$

for each i where $1 \leq i \leq n-1$. Note that the variable x_n does not appear in B_i's any more. Taking:

$$C_i(x_1, x_2, \cdots, x_{n-2}) = \text{res}(B_i, B_{n-1})$$

for each i where $1 \leq i \leq n-2$ it is seen that neither x_n nor x_{n-1} appear in C_i's. Continuing in this manner, one eventually obtains a polynomial, say, $Z_1(x_1) = 0$. By theorem 2.1, if $A_i(a_1, a_2, \cdots, a_n) = 0$ for $1 \leq i \leq n$, then clearly $Z_1(a_1) = 0$.

Similarly, one can compute $Z_2, Z_3, \cdots, Z_n$ such that $Z_2(a_2)=0$, $Z_3(a_3)=0$, $\cdots, Z_n(a_n)=0$ whenever $(a_1, a_2, \cdots, a_n)$ is a zero of the original system (i.e. $A_1=0$, $A_2=0$, $\cdots$, $A_n=0$).

Note that, if Z_i's are all nonzero polynomials then there are only a finite number of n-tuples $(a_1, a_2, \cdots, a_n)$ such that $Z_1(a_1)=0$, $Z_2(a_2)=0$, $\cdots$, $Z_n(a_n)=0$, and every solution of the given system will be among these n-tuples. Thus it is sufficient to find the roots of these univariate polynomials and then determine which n-tuples are solutions of the initial system. Heindel [1971] describes a system which employs Sturm's theorem [van der Waerden 1977] to calculate within any prespecified yet unlimited accuracy all the real zeros of a univariate polynomial, and this is exactly what is demanded since complex roots are not meaningful in our setting.

Although the above method is straightforward, there are some problems that make it difficult to implement in a computer for large values of n. The following theorem explains this:

THEOREM 2.2. Let R be a commutative ring with identity and let A and B be polynomials of positive degree over R. Then there exists polynomials S and T over R such that $AS+BT=\mathrm{res}(A,B)$ and $\deg S<\deg B$, $\deg T<\deg A$. (Here $\deg A$ denotes the degree of polynomial A.)

Proof. cf. Collins [1971]. $\square$

This means that $\mathrm{res}(A,B)$ can have powers up to $2\deg A \deg B$. Thus, in the above discussion about solving a system of equations, the final univariate polynomials Z_i may be in the worst case of order doubly-exponential in n. (There is certainly a similar growth in the size of the coefficients of the resultant but this is somewhat less important.)

It is thus admitted by experts [E. Kaltofen, private communication 1985] that elimination is very inefficient for solving a system of nonlinear equations even for small n. Thus, numerical methods may be desirable to solve the system in (3).

A classical method that is applicable is the Newton-Raphson method. Let J denote $n \times n$ Jacobian matrix defined by $J_{ij}=\nabla Q_i/\nabla x_j$. Then the $(r+1)$-st iteration of the Newton-Raphson method is given as:

$$X_{r+1}=X_r-Q(X_r)J^{-1}(X_r)$$

where the vectors X and Q are given as $X=(x_1 x_2 \cdots x_n)$ and

$Q=(Q_1Q_2\cdots Q_n)$. The convergence of the method is dependent on the initial estimate X_0. A typical feature of the method is that the number of correct significant digits roughly doubles at each iteration.

We have seen that purely algebraic schemes, such as elimination, may lead to severe performance penalties. Use of local methods, such as Newton-Raphson, can be a hit-or-miss process. In this case, continuation methods provide the best known technique for computing solutions to polynomial systems. It is noted however that continuation methods also run quite inefficiently. Morgan [1983] states that the run time of his SYMPOL system which is based on continuation is proportional to the "total degree" (the product of the degrees of the individual equations) of the system under investigation. A major advantage of the method is that it is not affected by the choice of initial estimates of solutions and is accordingly very reliable. Garcia and Zangwill [1981] is the definitive source on the subject of continuation. Garcia and Zangwill [1979] treat the case of solving polynomial equations using this method. Here we give an overview of the latter.

We want to solve the polynomial system $A_i(x_1,x_2,\cdots,x_n)=0$ where $1\leq i \leq n$, or written compactly, the system $A(x)=0$. We assume that we can solve $G(x)=0$, a "simplified" system to be specified below. We then form the homotopy:

$$H(x,t)=tA(x)+(1-t)G(x)$$

where $t\varepsilon[0,1]$, and generate a "flow" from the solutions of $G(x)=0$ to those of the original system by starting at *all* solutions for $t=0$ and following the corresponding paths until $t=1$. The details of how this is done are not particularly illuminating and will be omitted here. Let $c_1,c_2,\cdots,c_n$ be complex numbers and let $p(k)$ stand for $\deg A_k$. Then the k-th component of G will be defined as:

$$G_k=x_k^{1+p(k)}-c_k$$

The following theorem becomes very important:

THEOREM 2.3. If for all $x_0\varepsilon C^n$ (n-dimensional complex space) and $t_0\varepsilon[0,1]$ the statements:

(a) $A(x_0)=0$ implies $\det DA(x_0)\neq 0$

and

(b) $H(x_0, t_0) = 0$ implies rank$DH(x_0, t_0) = 0$

hold, then all solutions to $A(x) = 0$ can be found by the continuation process described above. (Here DH (respectively DA) is the $2n \times (2n+1)$ (respectively $2n \times 2n$) real matrix of partial derivatives of H (respectively A). The determinant of A is denoted by det$A$ whereas rank$A$ denotes its rank.)

Proof. cf. Garcia and Zangwill [1979]. $\Box$

One may inquire when the hypothesis of theorem 2.3 (i.e. conditions (a) and (b)) holds. The following result is thus relevant:

THEOREM 2.4. The set of all $(c_1, c_2, \cdots, c_n) \varepsilon C^n$ for which part (b) of the hypothesis of theorem 2.3 does not hold has measure zero in C^n.

Proof. A sketch is given by Morgan [1983]. $\Box$

The elegance of theorem 2.4 is that we can select $c_1, c_2, \cdots, c_n$ in random and reasonably expect them to satisfy the hypothesis of theorem 2.3, assuming that part (a) of it already holds. The method may lead to some "bad" paths which diverge to infinity. Since theorem 2.3 guarantees that each solution will have a convergent path this is not a theoretical deficiency; yet it may degrade the performance. In other words, theorem 2.3 generates $\prod_1^n (1 + p(i))$ paths whereas the maximum number of solutions is only $\prod_1^n p(i)$. We did not implement a continuation method although we are convinced that it may be one of the best available approaches to solve OPTIMAL LINE VISIT (but cf. section 6.2).

Until now, we summarized a way of solving OPTIMAL LINE VISIT based on the solution of a system of equations, either using purely algebraic techniques or numerical analysis. Another numeric method is to apply optimization. Consider the objective function:

$$D(x_1, x_2, \cdots, x_n) = \sum_0^n d(b_i, b_{i+1})$$

This is the total length of an s-to-g path with bend points b_i. To minimize D, we can use the formula:

$$X_{r+1} = X_r - G(X_r) H^{-1}(X_r)$$

where G is the gradient vector $(\nabla D / \nabla x_1 \nabla D / \nabla x_2 \cdots \nabla D / \nabla x_n)$ and H is the

$n \times n$ Hessian matrix defined by $H_{ij} = \nabla^2 D / \nabla x_i \nabla x_j$. Like Newton-Raphson method, the success of the optimization rests on the good selection of X_0.

We shall now consider the following variant of OPTIMAL LINE VISIT:

OPTIMAL EDGE VISIT

INSTANCE: Line segments $E = \{e_1, e_2, \cdots, e_n\}$ and points s, g, all situated in R^3. (Each line segment e_i is specified by its endpoints.)

QUESTION: What is the s-to-g shortest path constrained to pass through the sequence of line segments $e_1, e_2, \cdots, e_n$ in that order?

OPTIMAL EDGE VISIT requires the bend points of the shortest path to belong to the closure of the line segments; hence a direct application of OPTIMAL LINE VISIT to the lines defined by the given line segments will not in general provide the right answer. Nevertheless, we shall show that OPTIMAL EDGE VISIT is solvable after 3^n applications of OPTIMAL LINE VISIT to instances whose total individual size is n.

Denote the line carrying e_i by L_i (thus $L_i = \text{aff} e_i$) and apply OPTIMAL LINE VISIT to the resulting instance. If the bend points b_i of the path computed by OPTIMAL LINE VISIT are such that $b_i \varepsilon \text{cl} e_i$, $1 \leq i \leq n$, then we are done. Otherwise, some bend points of the computed path are external to some segments. In this case, it must be clear that the shortest path through the given edges will bend at at least one endpoint of the given edges at which point it will not subtend equal entry and exit angles, contrary to lemma 2.1.

Let the endpoints of edges e_i's be denoted by e_{i1} and e_{i2}. Let *combs* be the set of all combinations of length n where each combination is obtained by selecting one member from the following sets in the given order:

$\{L_1, e_{11}, e_{12}\}$

$\{L_2, e_{21}, e_{22}\}$

$\cdots$

$\{L_n, e_{n1}, e_{n2}\}$

Note that a given member of *combs* defines at most n subproblems that should be submitted to OPTIMAL LINE VISIT. The subproblems are simply obtained by isolating the parts of the given combination between consecutive pairs of endpoints. We shall now illustrate this:

EXAMPLE 2.1. Assuming that $n=7$ we should solve 3^7 problems, one for each combination. For instance, one of the combinations in *combs* is the following:

$$s, L_1, e_{21}, L_3, L_4, e_{52}, L_6, e_{71}, g$$

For this combination we must solve four subproblems as follows:

- Apply OPTIMAL LINE VISIT to instance s, L_1, e_{21}.
- Apply OPTIMAL LINE VISIT to instance e_{21}, L_3, L_4, e_{52}.
- Apply OPTIMAL LINE VISIT to instance e_{52}, L_6, e_{71}.
- Apply OPTIMAL LINE VISIT to instance e_{71}, g. This is a trivial instance. □

Note that if, during the application of OPTIMAL LINE VISIT to a subproblem, any of the found bend points turn out to be external to the given segments then we can abort the whole computation for this combination since it will be accounted for in a future combination. Once we are through with a combination, we add the lengths of the paths computed for the subproblems to arrive at the length of the shortest path for this particular combination. The combination which gives the shortest among the members of *combs* is chosen as the optimal one.

After all these preparations and remarks, we are now ready to give our algorithm to solve FINDPATH in its full generality:

ALGORITHM FINDPATH

1. Let $E = \bigcup_1^n edge P_i$ and let $EP = 2^E - \phi$ where 2^E denotes the power set of E. Let $\bar{C} = \phi$ and $\bar{l} = +\infty$.

2. Do the following steps for each permutation of each $T \varepsilon EP$:

   2.1. Compute the shortest path C by applying OPTIMAL EDGE VISIT to the instance made of the edges in T, and s and g.

   2.2. If C intersects any P_i's interior, then discard it and continue with step 2. (Here, we use a standard line segment-polyhedron intersection detection routine.) Otherwise, if $l(C) < \bar{l}$ then replace $\bar{C}$ by C and let $\bar{l} = l(\bar{C})$, and continue with step 2.

END

This algorithm gives one s-to-g shortest path $\overline{C}$ and its length $\overline{l}$. To obtain all s-to-g shortest paths, in case there are more than one, the following modifications can be made. Initialize a list of candidate shortest paths, $cands = \phi$, at step 1. When a path C is not discarded at step 2.2, let $cands = cands \cup C$ and skip the rest of step 2.2. Finally, we add a third step which sorts $cands$ in ascending order by path length and takes the initial portion of it containing the equal-length paths.

2.2. Efficiency Considerations

Assume temporarily that we have a black box which efficiently solves OPTIMAL EDGE VISIT problem numerically. Even in this case, our FINDPATH algorithm would be extremely inefficient since it tries all permutations (of any length) of edges to compute the shortest path. (Testing a path against the obstacles for intersection detection is subsumed by the root finding process - a reasonable assumption.) Since $n != \sqrt{2\pi n}\ (n/e)^n (1+O(1/n))$, the execution time of FINDPATH would still be dominated by $O(n^n)$. Currently there is no algorithm which provably does better than this bound. In other words, the best known algorithm for FINDPATH is nothing but the naive "try all possibilities" approach.

Needless to say, even the numerical solution of OPTIMAL LINE VISIT is nontrivial as we remarked in section 2.1. We shall give evidence that suggests that OPTIMAL LINE VISIT becomes intractable if we relax the requirement that the given lines should be visited in a prespecified order. To see this, assume the existence of a polynomial algorithm to solve unordered OPTIMAL LINE VISIT. We shall then show that one can use this as a subroutine to solve GEOMETRIC TRAVELING SALESMAN in polynomial time, a very unexpected result in the light of the fact that the latter is NP-complete in the strong sense both in the "tour" and the "path" versions [Papadimitriou 1977]. (In the path version, we are not required to come back to our starting point although we must still visit all the cities.)

For the demonstration, let the cities for GEOMETRIC TRAVELING SALESMAN (path) be the points $c_1, c_2, \cdots, c_n$ in the plane. Consider the lines passing through c_i's and perpendicular to this plane and denote them by $L_1, L_2, \cdots, L_n$. Since we assumed that OPTIMAL LINE VISIT (unordered) works in polynomial time, we are assured that for a given pair of cities which act as the source and the goal we can find a source-to-goal shortest path in 3-space efficiently. (This path, on the other hand, is obviously confined to the plane of c_i's.)

The path starts at the source, visits some permutation of $L_1, L_2, \cdots, L_n$, and ends at the goal. Since the number of such pairs is only $O(n^2)$, we can try all of them and select the one which gives the shortest path, which necessarily will be the shortest salesman path in the plane. The discrepancy follows. (N.B. This was a reduction "that proved nothing" [Johnson and Papadimitriou 1985].)

Returning to our discussion about the inefficiency of FINDPATH, it is seen that what we need is a quick way of deciding which permutations of edges are simply useless. If we can do this then all such permutations can be discarded without ever applying OPTIMAL EDGE VISIT on them. One may argue, from a complexity viewpoint, that it is probably useless to use such "trimming" strategies, but in practice they may help considerably, e.g. consider branch-and-bound techniques for accelerating the solution of NP-complete problems.

In the following assume that all members of P (the set of original polyhedra) are convex. Let $e_1, e_2, \cdots, e_k$ be a given sequence of edges in this environment. The first short-cut is obvious:

LEMMA 2.3. Let e_i, e_{i+1}, $1 \le i < k$, be two edges in the above sequence such that $e_i, e_{i+1} \varepsilon \text{edge} P_j$ for some $P_j \varepsilon P$. Let F_1 and F_2 be the lowest-indexed faces of P_j which hold e_i and e_{i+1}, respectively. If $F_1 \ne F_2$ then this sequence cannot contribute to the shortest path computation and can thus be discarded.

Proof. The convexity of P_j guarantees that there is no way to go from e_i to e_{i+1} without intersecting $\text{int} P_j$. $\square$

The second short-cut is as follows:

LEMMA 2.4. An s-to-g shortest path cannot pass through any member of $\bigcup_1^n \text{vert} P_i$. ($P_i$'s are still considered to be convex.)

Proof. If $\overline{C}$ is a shortest path on the boundary of a convex polyhedron $P_k \varepsilon P$, then Sharir and Schorr [1986] prove that $\overline{C}$ cannot pass through a vertex of P_k. We shall now extend this to the case of several convex polyhedra. If the shortest path $\overline{C}$ in this case first lands on a face of a polyhedron P_k, then visits a vertex v_j of it, and then takes off, then the their proof is certainly applicable without modification. Otherwise the situation is as shown in figure 2.2. Now consider two points on $\overline{C}$: point a in the ε-neighborhood of v_j but before it (along $\overline{C}$ when it is seen as a directed path extending from s to g), and point b in the ε-neighborhood of v_j but after it. Obviously a and b cannot see each other. Let P' be a small and appropriately chosen subset of P_k, including v_j and its say, $c\varepsilon$-neighborhood for a constant c, $0 < c < 1$. It is now possible to construct $\text{conv}(P' \cup \{a,b\})$ to compute a shorter path from a to b which at the same time avoids v_j. The contradiction follows. $\square$

This result is extensible to the case of arbitrary polyhedra but then we must be careful about the vertices where lemma 2.4 holds. Figure 2.3 shows a non-convex polyhedron with a "valley" which forces the s-to-g shortest path to pass through the vertices v_1 and v_2. It is thus seen that lemma 2.4 is in general correct only for convex (nonreflex) vertices.

The importance of lemma 2.4 is that it eliminates the need to perform OPTIMAL EDGE VISIT altogether in an exclusively convex environment. That is, if we perform a shortest path computation via OPTIMAL LINE VISIT on a sequence of edges in the presence of convex obstacles and find out that the path should pass through some vertices, then we can immediately discard this sequence.

Returning to lemma 2.3, can we find additional similar short-cuts? One such way would be to abandon a sequence which has two consecutive edges (belonging to possibly different polyhedra) which cannot "see" each other.

DEFINITION 2.1. Two edges e_1 and e_2 of a polyhedral scene $P = \{P_1, P_2, \cdots, P_n\}$ are (partly) *visible* from each other if there exists a point of e_1 visible to a point of e_2. Otherwise (when no such pair is possible), e_1 and e_2 are *invisible* from each other. $\square$

Note that if two edges are only partly visible from each other then an edge sequence holding them in consecutive order cannot in general be rejected by FINDPATH without further consideration. Definition 2.1 suggests the following decision problem:

EDGE-TO-EDGE VISIBILITY

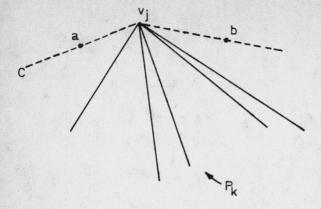

Figure 2.2 A shortest path cannot visit a convex vertex.

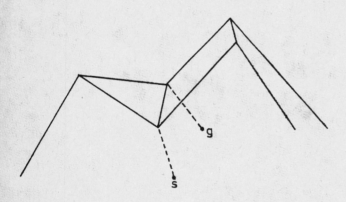

Figure 2.3 A shortest path can visit a nonconvex vertex.

INSTANCE: As in definition 2.1.

QUESTION: Are e_1 and e_2 invisible to each other?

To quote Papadimitriou [1985]: "This problem is quite intricate, despite its deceivingly simple statement." When we first posed it in [Akman 1985], we were not aware of an efficient algorithm to solve this problem. As a matter of fact, at that time, even the 2-dimensional version of the problem, where there are polygons with a total of m edges, did not possess a fast solution; this situation has changed after the recent discoveries by Toussaint and his coworkers [Toussaint 1985, Avis et al 1985] first of an $O(m \log m)$, and then an $O(m)$ and thus optimal algorithm.

A straightforward yet rather inefficient algorithm for 3-space would be to write down a logical formula in reals and would then be based upon employing the technique of Collins [1975] for satisfiability; see Reif and Storer [1985] for an example of how this is accomplished. Clearly, this approach does not take into account the geometric aspect of the problem and is not the right way to discover a fast algorithm.

From a geometric viewpoint, let H be the convex hull (a tetrahedron in general) of the given endpoints of the given line segments. Then e_1 and e_2 are invisible to each other if the object obtained by subtracting all polyhedra (P_i's) from H contains "walls" so as to block any line segment connecting a point of e_1 to a point of e_2. An obvious Monte-Carlo approach (which is vulnerable to an adversary) is to suitably choose point pairs, one belonging to e_1 and another to e_2, and to test the line segment connecting them against all polyhedra for intersection detection. If a prespecified number of trials are always concluded with reported intersections then we may argue that the given line segments are invisible to each other, with some degree of confidence.

The situation in 3-space is now settled by Papadimitriou [1985] who gives a $O(m^2)$ solution where m is the total number of edges. Implementation of the algorithm appears difficult since it makes use of intersecting hyperbolic regions and point-location within curved planar subdivisions; we shall however briefly summarize it. Let the lines L_1 and L_2 carrying the given edges be parametrized by λ_1 and λ_2. Denote the region of the $\lambda_1\lambda_2$-plane which represents pairs of points of the two lines visible from another by V. Points $\lambda_1 \varepsilon L_1$ and $\lambda_2 \varepsilon L_2$ are invisible from each other if and only if $\lambda_1\lambda_2 \cap T_i \neq \phi$ for some triangle T_i. (Assume, without loss of generality, that all polyhedral faces are triangulated.)

Let V_i consist of all (x,y)'s such that $xy \cap T_i = \phi$. Then $V = \overset{O(m)}{\underset{1}{\cap}} V_i$. Furthermore

it is possible to show that each V_i can be constructed in $O(1)$ time. Overall, by a naive approach, V can be found in time $O(m^2)$ and it turns out to be a planar graph with edges made of hyperbolic portions. Having found V, it is now conceptually straightforward to check whether the rectangle in the $\lambda_1\lambda_2$-plane of the segments intersects V. If it fails to intersect V, the corresponding segments are invisible from each other.

3. Solutions of Two Specific Instances of FINDPATH

This chapter has two sections. Both sections treat the case $P = \{P_1\}$ where P_1 is convex. (In the rest of the chapter we shall simply use P instead of P_1.) Section 3.1 details the case where $s, g \in \mathrm{bd}P$. Section 3.2 uses the solution for that case to solve the instance where s and g are both external to P.

3.1. Shortest Paths on a Convex Polyhedron

Consider the following highly restricted version of FINDPATH:

> BOUNDARY FINDPATH
>
> INSTANCE: Convex polyhedron P, specified points $s, g \in \mathrm{bd}P$ where $s \neq g$.
>
> QUESTION: Which s-to-g path $C \in \mathrm{bd}P$ has the shortest length?

Before we solve this problem we shall give an argument as to its importance. Let $P = \{P_1, P_2, \cdots, P_n\}$ be a set of *convex* polyhedra. If we are allowed to compute a reasonably short (but not the shortest) s-to-g path then we can pursue the following strategy. Let P' be the subset of P such that every member of P' is intersected by the segment sg. (If a polyhedron is intersected by sg only once then it is not included in P'; thus P' consists of polyhedra intersected by sg at precisely two points.)

Applying BOUNDARY FINDPATH to each member of P' we obtain an s-to-g polygonal path which comprises two types of curves: (i) Line segments through free space, and (ii) Polygonal paths along the boundaries of the polyhedra between where the path lands from free space and takes off again (figure 3.1). Repeated optimization of this path is now possible and will frequently yield a better (with fewer bend points) and shorter path (figure 3.2), although it is not difficult to come up with cases where such repeated optimization might cause clashes.

We shall assume throughout the book that a simple *boundary representation* is used to define a polyhedron P. In this representation scheme, each vertex is defined by its x, y, z coordinates and each face is given as a list of pointers to the vertices, ordered counterclockwise around the boundary of the face with respect to a point above it. It is convenient to think of vertex labels or face labels as positive integers.

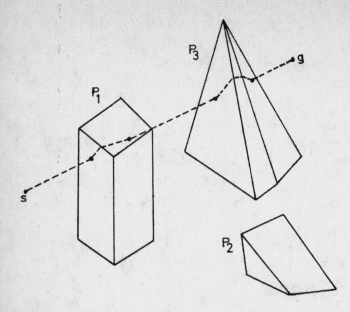

Figure 3.1 A reasonably short path between *s* and *g* in the presence of convex polyhedral obstacles.

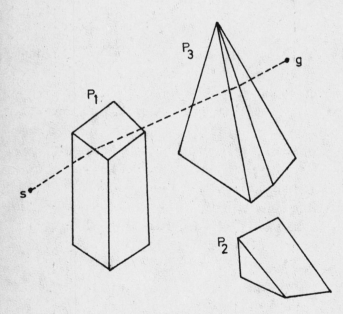

Figure 3.2 Further optimization of the path shown in figure 3.1 yields a shorter path with fewer bend points.

DEFINITION 3.1. The *face graph (Fgraph)* of a convex polyhedron P is an undirected graph $Fgraph = (FV, FE)$ with unit arc weight, $FV = \{i : F_i$ is a face of $P\}$ and $FE = \{(i,j) : F_i$ and F_j *are adjacent*$\}$. (Two faces are adjacent if they share an edge.) □

EXAMPLE 3.1. Figure 3.3(a) shows the face graph of a cube. In figure 3.3(b), the face graph of a parallelepiped is given to note that *Fgraph* only preserves the adjacency information. Figure 3.3(c) shows that two faces with a common point only are not considered adjacent by this definition. □

DEFINITION 3.2. Let $C \varepsilon bdP$ be an s-to-g polygonal path. The sequence of faces that C enters defines the *face visit sequence* of C. This will be denoted by $fvsC$. □

Thus $fvsC$ is a walk in *Fgraph* between the nodes corresponding to faces F_s and F_g, the faces of P containing s and g, respectively. An immediate consequence of the above definition is:

LEMMA 3.1. Let $\bar{C} \varepsilon bdP$ be an s-to-g shortest path. Then $fvs\bar{C}$ is a simple walk in *Fgraph* of P.

Proof. If this is not true then $\bar{C}$ enters a face of P at least twice. Recalling the fact that the faces of P are all convex, we can then further shorten $\bar{C}$, a contradiction. □

From now on, all face visit sequences will therefore be assumed to be simple. In addition to *Fgraph*, a useful construct that will be used by BOUNDARY FINDPATH is the planar development of a given face visit sequence. It is well-known that the boundary of a convex polyhedron has the structure of a planar graph. Therefore, the totality of the faces of P, situated in 3-space in certain mutual relationship, can be represented in 2-space (specifically the xy-plane) by a system of polygons identified with the faces of P. Frechet and Fan [1967] refer to this as the "planar polygonal schema" while Abelson and DiSessa [1982] prefer the term "atlas," noting the similarity of it to a road atlas. The relationship between a planar development and the planar polygonal schema will be apparent after the following description of how to obtain the latter.

In the xy-plane, associate with each face of P a polygon having the same metrical form. (Two polygons have the same *metrical form* if they can be made to coincide by translations and rotations.) Define the *glue* relationship between the pairs of edges of these polygons such that two glued edges come from the *same* edge of P. Figure 3.4 illustrates this for a cube. Clearly, each edge in the

37

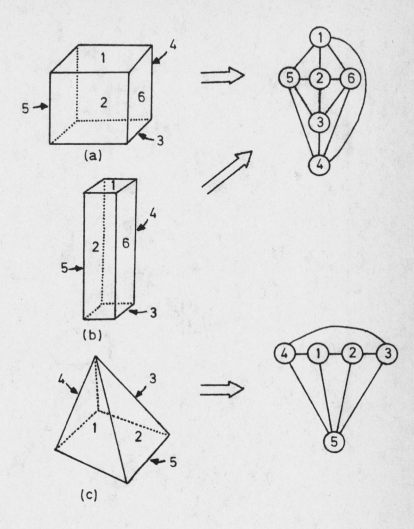

Figure 3.3 Face graphs of convex polyhedra:
(a) cube, (b) prism, (c) pyramid.

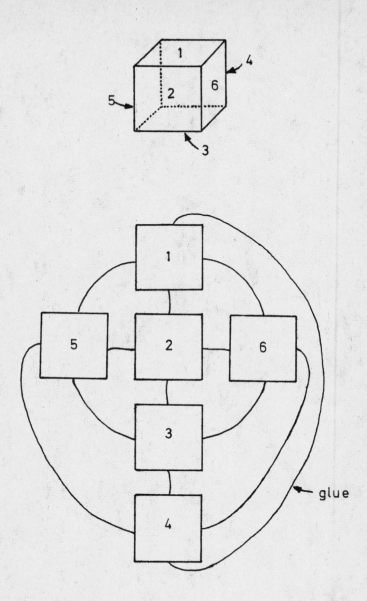

Figure 3.4 The planar polygonal schema of a cube.

planar polygonal schema is glued to exactly one edge.

DEFINITION 3.3. A *planar development* corresponding to a face visit sequence (generically denoted by $1,2,\cdots,k$) is a union of polygons $F_1,F_2,\cdots,F_k$ of the planar polygonal schema of P. In the planar development, two polygons F_i and F_{i+1}, $1 \leq i < k$, are united along the edge that they are glued to each other, and do not overlap. □

DEFINITION 3.4. The *image* of a point on a polyhedron under a planar development is the new point in the xy-plane that it ends up under the development. □

DEFINITION 3.5. A planar development is *legal* if the line segment connecting the images of the source and the goal points in the xy-plane is internal to the development. □

EXAMPLE 3.2. Figure 3.5 shows several planar developments computed and drawn by SP, our shortest path system to be described in chapter 5. The objects are as follows. Figure 3.5(a): cube, figure 3.5(b): icosahedron, figures 3.5(c) and (d): dodecahedron. It is noted that the last development is not legal. □

It should be apparent that once a planar development is built, it can be moved to any position and orientation in the plane without changing the *intrinsic geometry* (cf. [Alexandrov 1958, Efimov 1962]) of the paths. We shall now give a procedural definition of a planar development.

DEFINITION 3.6. (Also see definition 3.3) To compute the planar development of a face visit sequence $1,2,\cdots,k$, start with F_1. If affF_1 is parallel to the xy-plane then translate P by a suitable amount so that F_1 is now in the xy-plane; otherwise let the dihedral angle between affF_1 and the xy-plane be D and rotate P about the line, aff$F_1 \cap xy$-plane, by D to map F_1 to the xy-plane. The remaining faces F_i's are inductively handled as follows. Let e be the common edge of F_{i-1} and F_i whose dihedral angle is D. Rotate P by D about aff$e$ to place F_i to the xy-plane while avoiding overlaps with F_{i-1}'s polygon which is already there. □

After these definitions, we are ready for:

ALGORITHM BOUNDARY FINDPATH

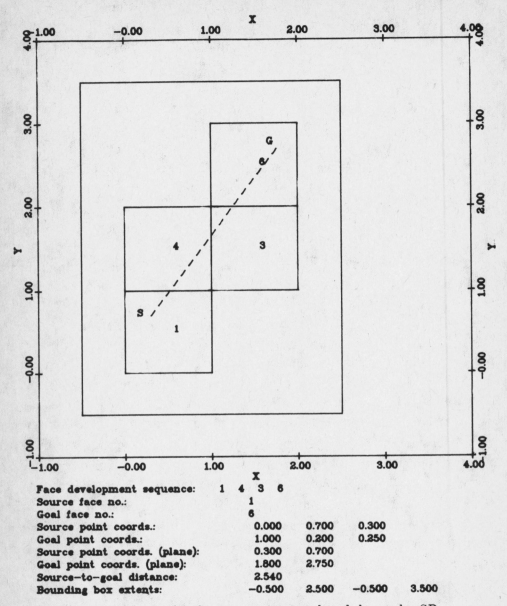

Face development sequence: 1   4   3   6
Source face no.:   1
Goal face no.:   6
Source point coords.:   0.000   0.700   0.300
Goal point coords.:   1.000   0.200   0.250
Source point coords. (plane): 0.300   0.700
Goal point coords. (plane):   1.800   2.750
Source—to—goal distance: 2.540
Bounding box extents: −0.500   2.500   −0.500   3.500

Figure 3.5 Some planar developments computed and drawn by SP.
The objects that are developed are as follows: (a) cube, (b)
icosahedron, (c) and (d) dodecahedron.

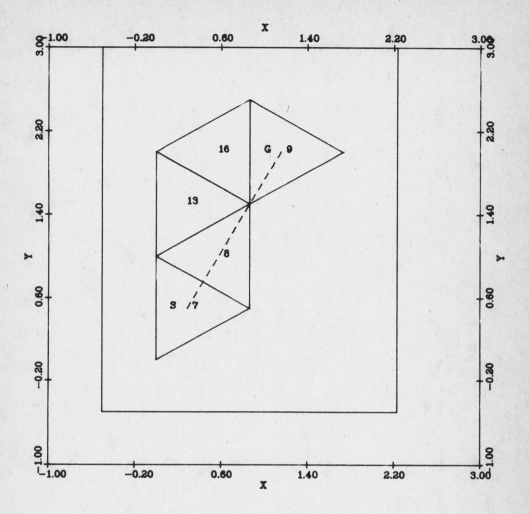

Face development sequence:7   8   13   16   9
Source face no.:   7
Goal face no.:   9
Source point coords.:   0.948   0.230   0.504
Goal point coords.:   0.192   1.206   0.504
Source point coords. (plane): 0.289   0.500
Goal point coords. (plane):   1.154   2.000
Source—to—goal distance: 1.732
Bounding box extents: −0.500   2.232   −0.500   3.000

(b)

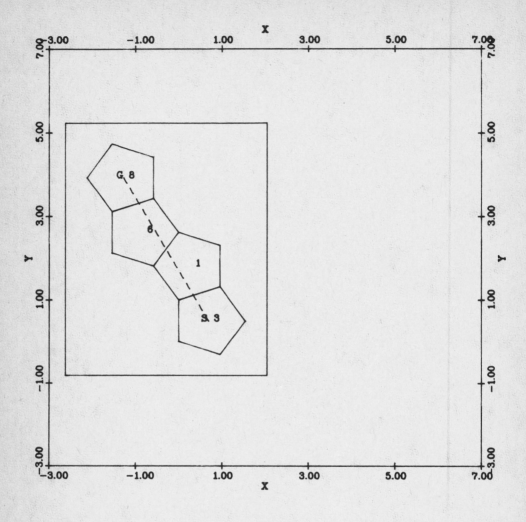

Face development sequence:	3	1	6	8
Source face no.:	3			
Goal face no.:	8			
Source point coords.:	0.380	1.447	0.616	
Goal point coords.:	0.996	−0.447	1.612	
Source point coords. (plane):	0.688	0.500		
Goal point coords. (plane):	−1.276	3.927		
Source−to−goal distance:	3.950			
Bounding box extents:	−2.627	2.039	−0.809	5.236

(c)

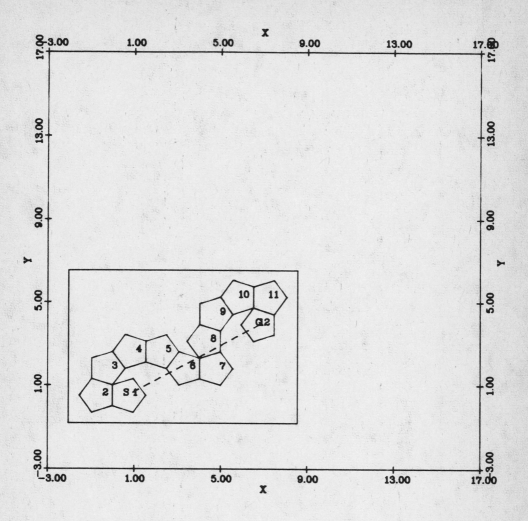

Face development sequence:	1	2	3	4	5	6	7	8	9	10	11	12
Source face no.:	1											
Goal face no.:	12											
Source point coords.:	0.688		0.500		0.000							
Goal point coords.:	0.688		0.500		2.227							
Source point coords. (plane):	0.688		0.500									
Goal point coords. (plane):	6.782		3.927									
Source-to-goal distance:	6.991											
Bounding box extents:	−2.039		8.558		−0.809		6.545					

(d)

1. Let F_s and F_g be the faces of P including s and g, respectively. Assume that $F_s \neq F_g$; otherwise the shortest path is found as $\overline{C} = sg$.

2. Let FVS be the set of all simple walks in $Fgraph$ of P, between the nodes corresponding to F_s and F_g. Initialize $\overline{vs} = \phi$ and $\overline{l} = +\infty$.

3. For each member (face visit sequence) of FVS do the following steps:

   3.1. Compute the planar development corresponding to this face visit sequence. Let s' and g' respectively be the images of s and g in the xy-plane under the same development. (As a practical observation, they can be computed along with the planar development itself.)

   3.2. If the development computed in step 3.1 is not legal then continue with step 3. Otherwise, if $d(s',g') < \overline{l}$ then replace $\overline{vs}$ by the current face visit sequence, let $\overline{l} = d(s',g')$ and continue with step 3.

4. At this point $\overline{l}$ is the length of the shortest path and $\overline{vs}$ is the face visit sequence that should be used to compute the shortest path itself. To do this, first compute the planar development of $\overline{vs}$ (and s' and g') and intersect the segment $s'g'$ with all pairwise common edges of the polygons in the development. The intersection points in the plane are then easily used to compute the bend points of the shortest path $\overline{C}$. Briefly, we know from the planar development of $\overline{vs}$ the distance of an intersection point from a vertex in the plane. All we need is to identify the vertex P in three dimensions that led to this vertex. Then marking the point which is away from this vertex the same distance over the edge touched by the shortest path, we locate the bend point for one intersection. The others are found completely analogously.

   END

An efficient way of checking whether a planar development is legal or not now follows. Let $e_1, e_2, \cdots, e_t$ be the sequence of edges that are glued in the development. Then the development is legal if $s'g'$ intersects every e_i. Note that this is always easier than testing if $s'g'$ is internal to the planar development's boundary.

To list the simple walks between two nodes of a graph we can use the algorithm of Yen [1971] which works in $O(kn^3)$ time if there are n nodes in the graph and we require the first k simple walks in increasing walk length. Katoh et al [1982] give an improved algorithm for the same task with a time complexity of $O(kf(n,m))$ under the assumption that shortest walks from one node to all others can be found in $f(n,m)$ time where m is the number of arcs in the graph. Since $f(n,m)$ is either $O(n^2)$ or $O(m\log n)$ in the worst case, this algorithm is more efficient than Yen's.

Determining the exact value of cardFVS is difficult. Garey and Johnson [1979] state that the following problem is NP-hard:

K-TH SHORTEST PATH

INSTANCE: Graph $G=(V,E)$, positive integer lengths l_e for each $e\,\varepsilon E$, specified nodes $s,t\,\varepsilon V$, and positive integers b and k.

QUESTION: Are there k or more distinct simple walks from s to t in G, each having length b or less?

They also mention that K-TH SHORTEST PATH remains NP-hard even if $l_e=1$ for all $e\,\varepsilon E$, and is solvable in pseudo-polynomial time (i.e. polynomial in card$V$, k, and $\log b$) and accordingly, in polynomial time for any fixed k. The difficulty of K-TH SHORTEST PATH basically resides in the following counting problem which was proven to be #P-complete by Valiant [1979]:

S-T PATHS (SELF-AVOIDING WALKS)

INSTANCE: Graph $G=(V,E)$ and specified nodes $s,t\,\varepsilon V$.

QUESTION: What is the number of walks from s to t that visit every node at most once?

Cartwright and Gleason [1966] give an algorithm to compute this number but their algorithm uses large matrices and is clearly impractical even for small values of card$V$.

The restricted problem of counting s-to-t walks in (s,t)-planar graphs is also #P-complete [Provan 1984]. (A graph is called *source-sink planar ((s,t)-planar)* if it has a planar representation with nodes s and t on the boundary.) Provan [private communication 1985] states that the approximation problem for (s,t)-walks is also unresolved in the sense that the following problem is open:

For any fixed $\varepsilon<1$, does there exist a polynomial algorithm which, for a given (s,t)-planar graph G, will give an approximation N_0 for the number N of (s,t)-walks in G such that $|N-N_0|<\varepsilon N$?

On the other hand, for any fixed $\varepsilon>0$, can it be proven that the above problem is NP-hard? Currently, the only known approximations are to count the minimum length walks or to enumerate as many walks as possible (using a large value of

k in Yen's algorithm, for example).

It is not hard to find a convex polyhedron which has an exponential number of simple walks in its *Fgraph* (figure 3.6). If there are l lateral faces of this pyramid-like object (not counting the small triangular faces) then the number of simple walks between the nodes F_s and F_g in the figure is $\Omega(2^{l/2})$. This result also shows that our BOUNDARY FINDPATH algorithm is of exponential time complexity in the number of faces of P in some cases. Section 4.3 will describe polynomial algorithms by other researchers for this problem. Unfortunately, these algorithms do not seem to admit practical implementations either. In the light of this, the algorithm presented in this section is applicable for objects of moderate complexity (number of faces). To make things faster, we can also try to test only a certain fraction (e.g. the first few in increasing walk length) of the face visit sequences between the source and the goal faces for an object with many faces, with the hope that the shortest path is generated by a short face development sequence. The shortest path rendered by the legal developments found among the developments that these sequences give may be taken as the true shortest path although this is certainly vulnerable to an adversary (figure 3.7).

3.2. Shortest Paths around a Convex Polyhedron

Now we inspect the following variant of BOUNDARY FINDPATH:

EXTERIOR FINDPATH

INSTANCE: Convex polyhedron P and noninterior points s,g where at least one of them is external to P, $s \neq g$.

QUESTION: Which $C \varepsilon C(s,g;P)$ has the shortest length?

Without loss of generality, we shall only treat the case where s and g are both outside P. In this case, the following is useful:

LEMMA 3.2. Let $H = \text{conv}(\{s,g\} \cup \text{vert} P)$. Then an s-to-g shortest path for EXTERIOR FINDPATH is entirely on bd$H$.

Proof. This can be proved in similar lines with the proof of theorem 1.1. $\square$

Thus, once H is computed using standard 3-space convex hull algorithms, we can apply BOUNDARY FINDPATH to the instance made of H, s, and g. (Preparata and Hong [1977] give an algorithm to find the 3-dimensional convex hull in time $O(n \log n)$ for n points.) However, there is a slight difficulty with this approach. Assuming that we want to know which edges of the original

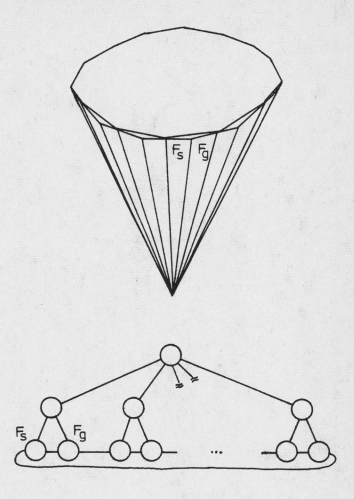

Figure 3.6 There exist an exponential number of simple walks between nodes F_s and F_g in *Fgraph* of this object.

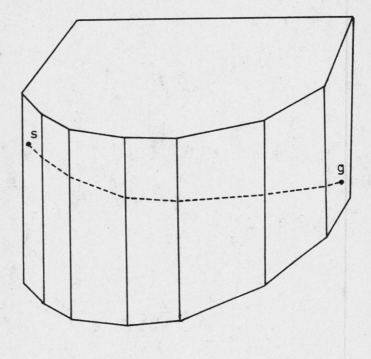

Figure 3.7 Shortest face visit sequences do not always render the shortest paths.

polyhedron the shortest path touches, we must keep extra information with H, i.e. which vertex of H comes from which vertex of P. Below, we shall give a more direct method to obtain H while keeping this information implicit using a visibility-based approach. (Sutherland et al [1974] give an excellent overview of polyhedral visibility.)

DEFINITION 3.7. For a convex polyhedron P and a point x external to it, the *silhouette edges* of P are members of

$$\{e : e \varepsilon F_1 \text{ and } e \varepsilon F_2 \text{ where } F_1 \varepsilon F_{vis} \text{ and } F_2 \varepsilon F_{invis}\}$$

Here, F_{vis} (respectively F_{invis}) is the set of visible (respectively invisible) faces of P from viewpoint x. □

Clearly, $F_{vis} \cap F_{invis} = \phi$ since a face of a convex polyhedron is either completely visible or completely hidden to an observer. Let $E_{sil,s}$ (respectively $E_{sil,g}$) denote the silhouette edges of P from s (respectively g). It is clear that the boundary of H will be the union of three disjoint (in fact they share edges) sets:

$$\text{bd}H = F_{tri,s} \cup F_{tri,g} \cup (F_{invis,s} \cap F_{invis,g})$$

Here $F_{tri,s}$ (respectively $F_{tri,g}$) is a set of triangular faces each characterized by an edge of $E_{sil,s}$ (respectively $E_{sil,g}$) and s (respectively g). In essence, these are the lateral faces of a pyramid-like object with (generally nonplanar) basis $E_{sil,s}$ (respectively $E_{sil,g}$) and apex s (respectively g). It is noted that the geometric complexity of object H is of the same order with P.

We conclude this section with an algorithm to compute the silhouette edges of P from a point x external to it:

ALGORITHM SILHOUETTE

1. Compute $F_{vis,x}$, the visible faces of P from viewpoint x, by checking line segments xc_i, where c_i is the center of mass of face F_i, against all F_j, $j \neq i$, for intersection. Thus $F_{vis,x}$ consists of all F_i's which do not cause any intersection.

2. Let the totality of the visible edges of P from x be $E_{vis,x} = \{e : e \varepsilon F \text{ where } F \varepsilon F_{vis,x}\}$. Sort $E_{vis,x}$ and eliminate *both* of the duplicate members in it. The remaining edges are precisely the edges of $E_{sil,x}$.

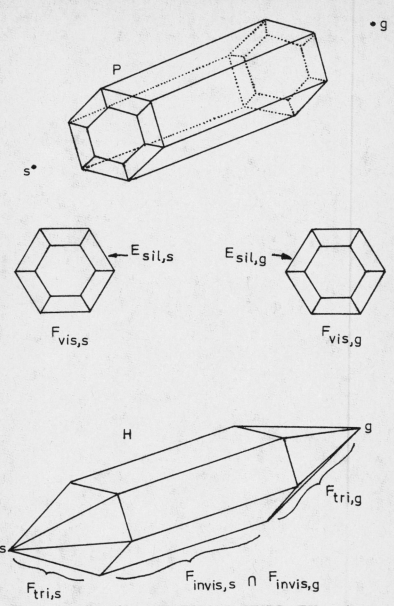

Figure 3.8 Demonstration of how EXTERIOR FINDPATH works via silhouettes.

END

Figure 3.8 demonstrates the working of EXTERIOR FINDPATH on a simple object. (In this example, we have chosen s and g in specific locations to make the picture easily imaginable for the reader.)

4. Two Voronoi-Based Techniques for FINDPATH

This chapter has three sections. In section 4.1 we introduce an extension of Voronoi diagrams on the boundary of a convex polyhedron and give an algorithm to compute it. Similarly, in section 4.2 we describe the partitioning of the free space around polyhedra into regions. Section 4.3 evaluates other 3-dimensional FINDPATH algorithms.

4.1. Partitioning the Boundary of a Convex Polyhedron

Consider the following variant of BOUNDARY FINDPATH:

BOUNDARY FINDPATH (locus)

INSTANCE: Same as in BOUNDARY FINDPATH, except that g is not given at the outset. However, it is guaranteed that, when specified, g will be on bd$P$.

QUESTION: Preprocess P so that for any specified $g \, \varepsilon \, \text{bd}P$ the s-to-g shortest path is computed efficiently.

A practical case which would benefit from BOUNDARY FINDPATH (locus) is as follows. Consider a truck on the surface of a mountain modeled as a convex polyhedron, say a pyramid. Suppose further that the truck is required to carry material from a fixed location on the surface to several points, say construction sites. Then it is reasonable to compute the shortest routes for the truck (which is approximated as a point) more efficiently than can be achieved by repeated applications of BOUNDARY FINDPATH for each destination.

This corresponds to a powerful paradigm of computational geometry known as the *locus approach* and is, for example, studied in Overmars [1983]. In solving a problem using this approach, we are allowed to spend some initial effort (i.e. preprocessing) to construct a data structure which will let us answer future requests (i.e. queries) quickly. To be effective, this approach assumes two things. First, the number of query points must be large to validate such an initial investment. Second, the data structure must embody succinctly the locus of the required solution and must enjoy the existence of a fast search procedure to retrieve it.

We shall now summarize one such data structure suitable for solving BOUNDARY FINDPATH (locus). The data structure is known as the *Voronoi diagram* and was first introduced to computational geometry by Shamos [1978]. Let $S = \{x_1, x_2, \cdots, x_n\}$ be a subset of R^2. For $1 \leq i \leq n$ let:

$$\text{regn} x_i = \{y : d(x_i, y) \leq d(x_j, y) \text{ for all } j\}$$

be the *Voronoi region* of point x_i. The Voronoi diagram of S, denoted by vor$S$, partitions the plane into card$S = n$ regions, one region for each member of S. The (open) Voronoi region of point x_i consists of all points of R^2 closer to x_i than any other point of S. For $1 \leq i, j \leq n$, letting:

$$H_{ij} = \{y : d(x_i, y) \leq d(x_j, y)\}$$

(H_{ij} is the halfspace defined by the perpendicular bisector of line segment $x_i x_j$), it is seen that for $i \neq j$, one has regn$x_i = \bigcap H_{ij}$. Thus, regnx_i is a convex polygonal region and vor$S$ is equal to the union of the boundaries of all regnx_i. For every vertex x of vor$S$ there are at least three points x_i, x_j, and x_k in S such that $d(x, x_i) = d(x, x_j) = d(x, x_k)$. The Voronoi diagram for a set of n points has at most $2(n-2)$ vertices and $3(n-2)$ edges [Mehlorn 1984].

The Voronoi diagram of a point set S with n members can be computed in time $O(n \log n)$ and this is optimal with respect to a wide range of computational models [Preparata and Shamos 1985, Shamos and Hoey 1975, Klee 1980]. Unfortunately, practical Voronoi programs which are both fast and reliable are difficult to write mainly due to the special cases that may occur in the diagram and that are to be handled precisely. Among the published algorithms, those by Avis and Bhattacharya [1983], Lee [1982], and Guibas and Stolfi [1985] seem to be more promising for practical use. On the other hand, it is possible to construct asymptotically slower implementations which handle special cases without much effort.

We now summarize how to search Voronoi diagrams in time logarithmic in the number of the edges m of the diagram, i.e. we cite methods which let one find the point $x \varepsilon S$ such that for a query point $y \varepsilon R^2$, the length $d(x, y)$ is minimum. The search methods we shall review are more general than searching Voronoi diagrams in that they are based on searching a *planar subdivision* i.e. a straight-edge embedding of a planar graph. The underlying problem is generally known as *planar point-location* in computational geometry. Let us call a subset of the plane *monotone* if its intersection with any line parallel to the y-axis is a single (possibly empty) interval. A subdivision is monotone if all its regions are monotone. Mehlorn [1984] shows that a *simple* planar subdivision (a subdivision with only triangular faces) can be searched in time $O(\log m)$ after spending preprocessing time $O(m)$ and storage space $O(m)$. He also gives the following property to show that the situation is extensible to the case of *generalized* subdivisions, with a small penalty in preprocessing time:

LEMMA 4.1. If the searching problem for simple planar subdivisions with m edges can be solved with search time $O(\log m)$, preprocessing $O(m)$, and space $O(m)$, then the searching problem for general subdivisions with m edges can be solved with the same search time and space but preprocessing $O(m\log m)$. If all faces of the generalized subdivision are convex then $O(m)$ preprocessing is sufficient.

Proof. cf. Mehlorn [1984]. (Lee and Preparata [1977] also show that an arbitrary subdivision with m edges can be refined to a monotone subdivision having at most $2m$ edges in $O(m\log m)$ time.) □

We shall now review some planar point-location algorithms in the literature which either achieve these bounds or come close. Dobkin and Lipton [1976] were the pioneers to obtain the $O(\log m)$ query time but they use $O(m^2)$ space. Preparata [1981] modifies their method to prove that $O(m\log m)$ space is sufficient. His solution is implementable. In an important paper, Lee and Preparata [1977] give an algorithm which is based on the construction of separating chains. Their algorithm achieves $O(m\log m)$ preprocessing and $O(m)$ space bounds yet has a query time of $(\log^2 m)$. The constants hidden in these expressions are small and make their algorithm practically useful. (Their algorithm works for monotone subdivisions only.) Edelsbrunner and Maurer [1981] give a space-optimal solution which works for generalized subdivisions (and even for families of nonoverlapping subdivisions). Their query time is $O(\log^3 m)$. Lipton and Tarjan [1979, 1980] give a method with $O(\log m)$ query time and $O(m)$ preprocessing and space bounds (and thus optimal in all respects). Although based on a brilliant graph separator theorem which has many far-reaching consequences, they admit that their method is of only theoretical interest because of the serious implementation difficulties. Kirkpatrick [1983] gives another method with the same bounds. His method builds a hierarchy of subdivisions and seems to be easily implementable. Finally, Edelsbrunner et al [1986] give a substantial improvement of the technique of Lee and Preparata [1977] and again attain optimal bounds in all respects. The importance of their method is that it seems to admit an efficient implementation along with extensibility to subdivisions with curved edges.

Now we are in a position to present our algorithm for BOUNDARY FINDPATH (locus). In the following we shall show the partitioning for only a face (other than F_s) of P which we shall denote by F_g. To partition the whole bd$P$, we apply the following algorithm for each face. (Note that no partitioning is necessary for F_s due to convexity.)

ALGORITHM BOUNDARY FINDPATH (locus): Preprocessing

1. Find all simple face visit sequences between F_s and F_g using the *Fgraph* of P.

2. For each face visit sequence found in step 1, compute the image of s with respect to the planar development which starts with face F_g and ends with F_s. (Note that we are not required to compute the whole development itself, but just the image point.)

3. Compute the Voronoi diagram of the image points calculated in step 2 using standard Voronoi programs mentioned above. It is required that with each image point (Voronoi center) we store the face visit sequence which is used to arrive it.

4. Clip the diagram obtained in step 3 with respect to "window" F_g so as to preserve only those parts of it within polygon F_g. (Any of the standard graphics algorithm such as the one due to Sutherland and Hodge [Foley and van Dam 1982] can be used for clipping.)

END

Assume that for a given P, the above preprocessing is carried out for all faces (except F_s). Thus, we have a family of planar subdivisions for each face such that, for each region of a subdivision, we know the ordered sequence of faces to be developed to the plane if g is specified within that region. Specifically, we can apply the following algorithm when we are queried with a new g:

ALGORITHM BOUNDARY FINDPATH (locus): Querying

1. Compute the face F_g holding a given g. If $F_s = F_g$ then the shortest path is trivially sg.

2. Using the standard planar point-location algorithms mentioned above, locate g inside the planar subdivision belonging to F_g.

3. Since we stored the face development sequence used to arrive this region, we can now use it to compute the s-to-g shortest path. Note that there may be cases where g will be shared by at least two regions and thus there will be at least two shortest paths each of which is obtained via a different development sequence.

    END

Figure 4.1 shows the Voronoi partitioning on a face of a cube using the above algorithm. This figure was drawn by SP. It is noted that in figure 4.1(a), the given face is partitioned into four regions whereas in figure 4.1(b) this number becomes six. This effect was obtained by simply moving the source point to another location on the source face.

In general, the number of regions a given face F_g is partitioned by this algorithm is expected to be small. An informal argument for this is as follows. Consider the images of s in the plane of F_g. If the face visit sequence for a particular image is long then the image will usually end up in a point farther away from F_g compared to another image obtained by a shorter visit sequence. Thus, only a small portion of the possible face visit sequences between F_s and F_g can render images in the plane close to F_g and contribute to the Voronoi diagram on it.

4.2. Partitioning the Free Space around Polyhedra

The inspiration for the work to be described in this section is Franklin's [1982] extension of Voronoi diagrams in the plane in the presence of barriers (line segments). Here he generalizes the Voronoi concept by allowing opaque barriers that a shortest path must avoid. Within this environment, a shortest path will always be a polygonal path through the free space bending at the endpoints of the barriers. The ordered list of endpoints that a shortest path will pass through is called its *contact list*.

Franklin's construction works as follows. Regions are constructed so that every goal point in a region has a shortest path to the source with *identical* contact lists. Each region will have an *associated vertex* which is defined as the first vertex on its contact list. When a new barrier is introduced to the environment, two halflines (rays) extending from its endpoints are added. These boundaries are called the *shadow lines* and are the projections of the endpoints by the associated vertex of the region it is in. A second type of boundary is added to separate the

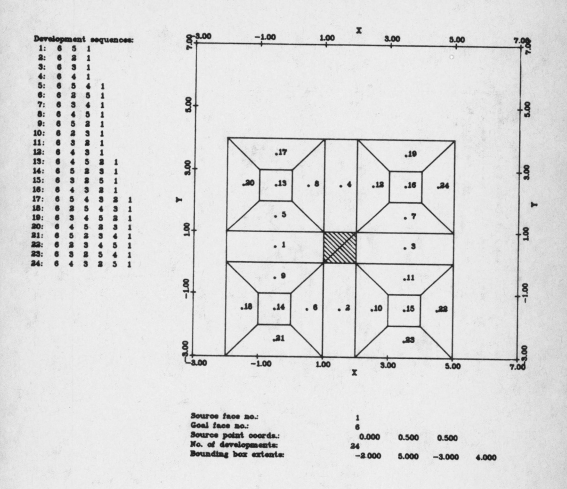

Figure 4.1 Demonstration of BOUNDARY FINDPATH (locus) on
a face of a cube. In figure 4.1(a) there are 4 regions on the goal
face (the shaded polygon) as a result of Voronoi partitioning. Figure 4.1(b) shows the effect of moving the source on the source face
to another location.

58

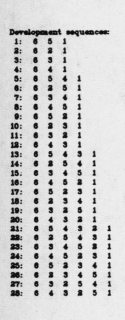

Development sequences:

1:	6	5	1			
2:	6	2	1			
3:	6	3	1			
4:	6	4	1			
5:	6	5	4	1		
6:	6	2	5	1		
7:	6	3	4	1		
8:	6	4	5	1		
9:	6	5	2	1		
10:	6	2	3	1		
11:	6	3	2	1		
12:	6	4	3	1		
13:	6	5	4	3	1	
14:	6	2	5	4	1	
15:	6	3	4	5	1	
16:	6	4	5	2	1	
17:	6	5	2	3	1	
18:	6	2	3	4	1	
19:	6	3	2	5	1	
20:	6	4	3	2	1	
21:	6	5	4	3	2	1
22:	6	2	5	4	3	1
23:	6	3	4	5	2	1
24:	6	4	5	2	3	1
25:	6	5	2	3	4	1
26:	6	2	3	4	5	1
27:	6	3	2	5	4	1
28:	6	4	3	2	5	1

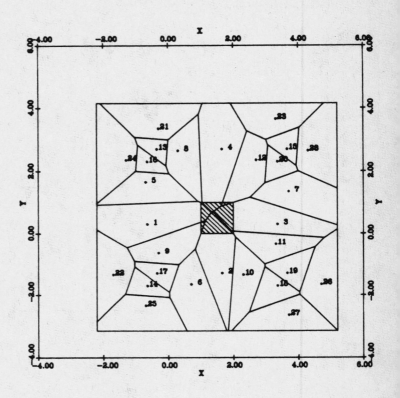

Source face no.:	1		
Goal face no.:	6		
Source point coords.:	0.000	0.300	0.650
No. of developments:	28		
Bounding box extents:	-2.200	5.200	-3.150	4.150

(b)

two new regions created. This will in general be a hyperbolic piece and is called the *ridge curve*. A goal on a ridge curve has two shortest paths to the source. If a boundary extends to the infinity nothing interesting happens. However, sometimes a boundary intersects a barrier or another boundary. In the former case, the boundary is *cut* (i.e. stops at or blocked by the barrier). In the latter case, when two boundaries hit each other they join to create a *junction*.

We shall now give an example to illustrate Franklin's partitioning. The reader is referred to [Verrilli 1984, Franklin et al 1985] for a complete implementation and several interesting computer-generated examples.

EXAMPLE 4.1. In figure 4.2, there are two barriers, ab and cd in the plane and s is given as shown in the figure. In this case the plane is partitioned into five regions. The region R_ϕ holds the goals directly reachable (visible) from s. The region R_a holds the goals which cause a shortest path to bend at the endpoint a of ab. The region R_b holds the goals which cause a shortest path to bend at b. R_d holds points which give rise to shortest paths bending at d. Finally, R_{ac} describes shortest paths bending first at a, and then at c while going from s to g. It can easily be shown that the boundaries between R_a and R_b, and R_d and R_{ac} are hyperbolic portions. All other boundaries are made of straight lines. □

A crucial property of the diagram in figure 4.2 (and of any similar partitioning in 2-space around barriers) is that a bend point *acts* as a source point for a later region. (For instance, a acts as a source for the points of region R_{ac}.) Thus the source is continuously "pushed back" and this is the underlying reason for all boundaries being either line segments or hyperbolic sections.

We now emulate Franklin's approach in 3-space where the regions will have the following property: all points of a given region are reached from the source after bending at the *same* edges of the obstructions in the *same* order. We shall call the problem naturally arising from the this definition FINDPATH (locus). Our treatment will not be algorithmic since we have not yet answered all the questions posed by this problem. In this environment, it is seen that the analogous constructs to those outlined above for 2-space will respectively be *associated edge*, *shadow plane*, and *ridge surface*. A *contact list* will now hold the ordered set of edges instead of endpoints. We shall use the terms *cut* and *junction* without modification, although they now refer to surfaces rather than curves.

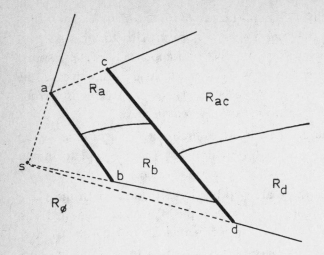

Figure 4.2 Franklin's partitioning in 2-space in the presence of
linear barriers.

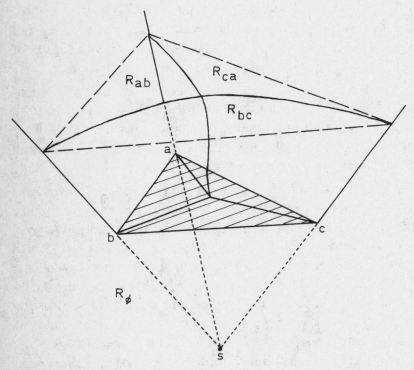

Figure 4.3 Partitioning the space in the presence of a solid triangle.

Let $a,b,c \in R^3$ be three noncollinear points. We shall denote the opaque triangle abc by T. Let s be any point outside aff$T$. We shall start with the following problem: partition the space into regions such that if a new $g \in R^3$ is specified, then we can tell if g can directly be reached from s, and if not, the edge of T where an s-to-g shortest path bends.

When g is outside the infinite frustum obtained by subtracting the finite pyramid described by basis T and apex s from the infinite pyramid described similarly, the shortest path is sg itself. Thus one of the regions, R_ϕ all points $g \in R^3$ such that $sg \cap T = \phi$. (In other words, R_ϕ is the set of all points visible from s.) If g is not in R_ϕ then three possibilities exist. For all $g \in R_{bc}$ the shortest path bends at bc. For all $g \in R_{ca}$ it bends at ca. Finally, for all $g \in R_{ab}$ it bends at ab. Accordingly, the edges bc, ca, and ab are the associated edges of the regions R_{bc}, R_{ca}, and R_{ab}, respectively. Figure 4.3 shows these regions. Intersections of R_ϕ with these three regions are the shadow planes for this example.

Now we shall compute the intersections of the pairs of regions. (These will be the ridge surfaces.) For clarity, we take s as the origin of the coordinate system without loss of generality. We shall compute the intersection of regions r_{ab} and R_{bc}, which then will be generalized to the other two cases. If $g \in R_{ab} \cap R_{bc}$ then there exists a shortest path to g either via ab or via bc. Label the bend points of this shortest path on ab (respectively bc) by d_{ab} (respectively d_{bc}). These points should satisfy:

$$d(s,d_{ab}) + d(d_{ab},g) = d(s,d_{bc}) + d(d_{bc},g) \tag{1}$$

The left (respectively right) hand side of (1) is equal to $d(s,g_{ab})$ (respectively $d(s,g_{bc})$) where g_{ab} (respectively g_{bc}) is the point obtained by rotating g about affab (respectively affbc) until it coincides with affsab (respectively affsbc) and is in the opposite halfplane with respect to s. In the sequel, we shall call any such point obtained by rotating a point about an axis an *image* point. If p is a point in 3-space and p' is its image due to rotation by an angle Θ about an axis u passing through the origin then it is well-known from computer graphics that:

$$p' = <p,u> + (p - <p,u>u)\cos\Theta + (u \times p)\sin\Theta \tag{2}$$

Applying (2) for the image of g about axis affab, we obtain:

$$g_{ab} = a + fu_{ab} + (ag - fu_{ab})\cos\alpha + (u_{ab} \times ag)\sin\alpha \tag{3}$$

where α is the dihedral angle between affsab and affgab, $u_{ab}=ab/d(a,b)$, and $f=<ag,u_{ab}>$. After some simplifications in (3), which are given in full in [Franklin and Akman 1985], the following expression for g_{ab} is obtained:

$$d^2(g_{ab})=d^2(a)+d^2(a,g)+2(<ag,u_{ab}><a,u_{ab}>+d(ag \times u_{ab})d(a \times u_{ab})) \tag{4}$$

To have a geometric interpretation of (4), we expand the scalar and the vector products in it and simplify the resulting expression to get:

$$d^2(g_{ab})=d^2(a)+d^2(ag)-2d(a)d(ag)\cos(\alpha_1+\alpha_2) \tag{5}$$

Here α_1 and α_2 are the angles $<gab$ and $<sab$, respectively (figure 4.4). Thus (5) is a statement of the *cosine theorem* for triangle sag_{ab}.

Up to this point, we have found an equation (i.e. (4)) that gives $d^2(g_{ab})$ in terms of known quantities a and u_{ab}, and unknown g. The corresponding equations for $d^2(g_{bc})$ and $d^2(g_{ca})$ are found completely analogously, with obvious modifications.

To compute the intersection of R_{ab} and R_{bc}, we must solve the equation $d(g_{ab})-d(g_{bc})=0$, or equivalently, $d^2(g_{ab})-d^2(g_{bc})=0$. In [Franklin and Akman 1985] we show that the intersection surfaces are in general ternary (in x,y,z which are the coordinates of g) quartics which may degenerate to planes in some cases. In the same reference we give a numerical example to illustrate the computation of the common surfaces using the above formulas.

If we want to partition the space behind a solid polygon instead of a triangle then we are required to compute all the potential boundaries between the pairs of regions. It is obvious that the intersections of the regions with the polygon (or the triangle for that matter) are made of straight edges. In fact the subdivision of the (back face) of the polygon by these edges can be found more simply:

LEMMA 4.2. Let P be a convex polygon with vertices $v_1,v_2, \cdots ,v_n$ and let s be a point outside aff$P$. The invisible side of P from s is partitioned into at most n convex regions (each completely containing an edge of P) such that for a goal g specified inside one of the convex regions the s-to-g shortest path is via the associated edge of this region.

Proof. We give a constructive proof which is entirely based on the technique employed in BOUNDARY FINDPATH (locus) (figure 4.5). Rotate s about affv_1v_2, affv_2v_3, $\cdots$,affv_nv_1 until it is coincident to aff$P$ and always on

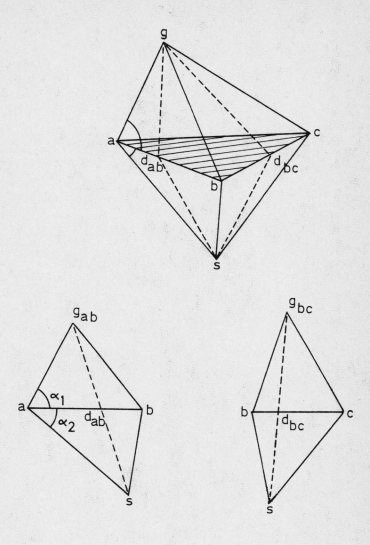

Figure 4.4 Computation of the images g_{ab} and g_{bc} of g.

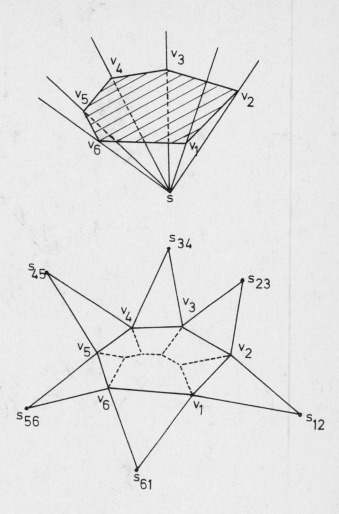

Figure 4.5 Voronoi partitioning on the back face of
an opaque polygon.

the opposite side of a particular edge with respect to int$P$. This is basically a planar polygonal schema of the pyramid with basis P and apex s, in the plane aff$P$. Denote the n image points obtained in this way by $s_{12}, s_{23}, \cdots, s_{n1}$ and construct the Voronoi diagram of these points. When clipped by the window P, the diagram partitions P into at most n regions which are necessarily convex since P is convex. $\square$

The extension of the above technique outlined for FINDPATH (locus) in the case of a single triangle to several obstacles creates difficult problems. In this case we cannot find a property similar to that of Franklin's partitioning mentioned above, i.e. the regions of the partition no more stay as quartics grow in degree for each new obstacle causing new regions. It is possible (although not easy) to determine how new regions will be formed as long as we have a picture of the workspace in front of us; however, we do not know an algorithmic way of doing this just from a description of the workspace. (This is yet another case where visual information is deemed essential.) In any case, building a rather elaborate version of Verrilli's [1984] system for 3-space, it is feasible to create the regions one by one for each new obstacle introduced to the workspace.

We shall now imagine that for a given s we managed to compute a subdivision of the free space into n regions bounded either by planes or quartic or higher-order surfaces, using the above approach. With each region we assume the existence of a stored "label" which is simply equal to the contact list for this region. If we are now given a new point g, we should first locate the region that g is in, and then use the associated contact list for this region to determine the s-to-g shortest path. Since the latter operation can be done using OPTIMAL EDGE VISIT we shall concentrate on the former problem.

Let S be a family of n planes in R^3. Dobkin and Lipton [1976] show how to represent S in a polynomial amount of space so that whether a given point belongs to any of the given planes can be tested in $O(\log n)$ time. If we approximate curved boundaries of our regions obtained above with planes then their algorithm is applicable. However, at least from a theoretical viewpoint, the need for such an approximation is not warranted since Chazelle [1984] generalizes Dobkin and Lipton's problem for the case where S is a family of algebraic varieties. His algorithm is an adaptation of Collins' [1975] quantifier elimination procedure. Let d be a positive constant and let $S = \{Q_1, Q_2, \cdots, Q_n\}$ be a set of polynomials of degree at most d in three variables with rational coefficients. (Thus, in our case d will be the degree of the highest-order surface in the partition.) Chazelle considers the problem of preprocessing S so that, for any $(x,y,z) \epsilon R^3$, the predicate:

There exists an i, $1 \leq i \leq n$, such that $Q_i(x,y,z) = 0$

can be evaluated efficiently. (This problem and its generalization to spaces higher than R^3 is known as *spatial point-location* in computational geometry.) If the predicate is true then any of the indices i for which $Q_i(x,y,z) = 0$ will be reported. Otherwise, (x,y,z) is seen to lie in a region over which each Q_i has a constant sign. Assuming that these regions have unique associated labels (which would be true by construction), Chazelle's algorithm retrieves the label corresponding to the region containing (x,y,z). The algorithm uses $O(n^{512})$ space and preprocessing time and computes each such predicate in time ($O \log n$). Although it completely meets our requirements to solve FINDPATH (locus), the possibility of a practical implementation of Chazelle's method is highly questionable.

4.3. Critique of Recent Algorithms for 3-Space

Among other works on shortest paths in 3-space, Sharir and Schorr's [1986] paper is the most detailed. They mainly consider the case of BOUNDARY FINDPATH (locus) and present an algorithm which works in time $O(n)$ per query where n is the measure of complexity of the polyhedron at hand, say the number of vertices. Their algorithm is based on the idea of "ridge" points on the object. A ridge point on the polyhedron has the property that there exists at least two shortest paths to it from the source. It turns out that the set of ridge points is a union of line segments and that the union of the vertices and the ridge points is a closed connected set. Defining the union of the latter with the shortest paths from the source to every vertex, one partitions the polyhedron's boundary into disjoint connected regions called "peels" whose interiors are free of vertices and ridge points. The peels can be constructed in time $O(n^3 \log n)$ (preprocessing) using complicated techniques whose implementation seems extremely difficult. The size of the data structure created by the preprocessing step is $O(n^2)$.

O'Rourke et al [1985] use most of Sharir and Schorr's ideas to extend the problem to a polyhedral surface which is no more supposed to be convex. (However it should be orientable.) The shortest path they calculate is only a geo-desic, i.e. it is confined to the surface and thus is not the true shortest path in many cases. Furthermore, their algorithm runs in time $O(n^5)$. Another weak point of the algorithm is that it does not follow a locus approach; using their algorithm on each new query (goal point) would take $O(n^4)$ time.

Mitchell et al [1985] give an algorithm to solve this last problem in a locus setting. (It is noted that they are still computing geodesics, not true shortest paths.) Theirs is an $O(n^2 \log n)$ time and linear space algorithm for subdividing the surface of an arbitrary polyhedron (possibly of nonzero genus) so that the length of the shortest path from a given source to any goal on the surface is obtainable by simple point-location. This method has striking similarities to Dijkstra's method for shortest paths in graphs. As in our algorithm presented in section 4.1, point-location is achieved in time $O(\log n)$, after which the actual shortest path is backtracked in time proportional to the number of faces that it traverses on the boundary. (Mount [1986] has extended these results to the case of multiple (say r) source points. He builds the partition of the boundary in time $O(N^2 \log N)$ where $N = \max(n, r)$.)

Mitchell and Papadimitriou [1985] pose a realistic version of the shortest path problem that they call "weighted region" problem. This is motivated by certain problem arising in terrain navigation where a robot must move at different speeds in different types of terrain [Mitchell and Papadimitriou July 1985]. In such a problem, one is given a polygonal subdivision of a 2-dimensional manifold in 3-space. Each region (or triangle, without loss of generality) has an associated integer weight. The length of a path is found as the weighted sum of the subpaths through each triangle. The special case of all weights belonging to $\{1, \infty\}$ is equivalent to the usual shortest path problem. To solve the problem they again apply a continuous Dijkstra technique: they imagine an "expanding wavefront" moving out from the source point and record the effects of the discrete events imposing critical changes on it. For n vertices, the time complexity of the algorithm is $O(n^3 L \log n)$ where L is the number of bits required to specify the largest number among the weights and the vertex coordinates.

Reif and Storer [1985] introduce the notion of "islands" in shortest path computation. For 2-dimensions, an island is defined to be a connected component of the obstacle space. For 3-space, an island is defined to be a maximal convex obstacle surface such that for any two points contained in the island, the shortest path between them is also within the island. Thus, k convex and disjoint polyhedra constitute k islands; a single nonconvex polyhedron constitutes *more than one* island. Let n be the total number of vertices and k be the number of islands. For 3-space they give an algorithm that runs in $O(n^{k^{O(1)}})$ time and another one that consumes $O(n^{\log k})$ space. Both algorithms are based on applications of Collins' [1975] theorem which states that a formula in the theory of real closed fields can be checked for satisfiability in time $O(dm^{2^{O(r)}})$ if it has length m, degree d, and r quantifiers. Reif and Storer also give another algorithm for 2-space which runs in preprocessing time $O(n(k+\log n))$ and query time $O(\log n)$.

Papadimitriou [1985] deals with the approximation of shortest paths. Given an instance of FINDPATH, he finds a path which is guaranteed to be at most $(1+\varepsilon)$ times the length of the shortest path in time that is polynomial in the size of the instance and ε^{-1}. (Thus it is a "fully-polynomial approximation scheme.") The basic idea of the algorithm is to break the edges of the given polyhedra into short segments in a nontrivial way. In other words, these new segments are such that the distance between two points on two segments can be taken constant independent of their relative position of them within the segments and the relative error thus introduced is not more than ε. The complexity of Papadimitriou's algorithm is $O(n^4\varepsilon^{-2}(L+\log(n/\varepsilon))^2)$; here L is the precision of the integers used (the number of bits in the largest integer describing the coordinates of the workspace element). A better way to understand this bound is to define $K=L+\log(n/\varepsilon)$; this corresponds to the precision of the instance since it contains the number of leading zero bits in ε in addition to the logarithms of n and the largest integer used. Papadimitriou also hints that it is possible to improve this bound to $O(n^3\varepsilon^{-1}K^2)$ using complicated techniques.

Bajaj [June 1985, July 1985, July 1986, March 1986] deals with algebraic issues posed by the shortest path problem. He points out that the problem of finding the shortest path between two points in 3-space bounded by a collection of polyhedral obstacles is not solvable by *radicals* over Q. To demonstrate this intuitively clear result, he generates the minimal polynomial whose root over the field Q is the solution to the shortest path problem. He then shows that the generated polynomial is minimal (by confirming it irreducible over Q) and uses Galois theory [van der Waerden 1977] to prove the polynomial to be not solvable by examining the structure of its Galois group. (For special relative orientations of the obstacles, the shortest path is straight-edge- and compass-constructible.) The meaning of this outcome is that there cannot exist *exact* algorithms for 3-dimensional unobstructed shortest paths under models of computation which only allow arithmetic operations and root extractions. Bajaj [April 1986] describes an obvious parallel solution for OPTIMAL LINE VISIT (ordered). (The idea of parallel methods for the shortest path problem is due to an insightful remark by Papadimitriou [1985].) His approach is to employ a parallel numerical iterative method running on a concurrent-read exclusive-write synchronous shared-memory model. The iterations are essentially Gauss-Seidel.

5. Desirable Functionalities of a Geometer's Workbench

This chapter has two sections. In section 5.1 we offer an overview of the desirable features of a geometer's workbench. Section 5.2 makes an initial attempt to put these ideas into a practical context by studying SP, our shortest path calculator.

5.1. General Considerations

One of the most exciting recent developments in computer graphics is the emergence of powerful workstations. Access to the computing power and the graphics facilities embedded in these machines is revolutionizing the way research is being done. In this section we shall discuss the functionalities expected from such workstations equipped with software to perform computational geometry, perhaps the closest branch of mathematics to profit from the existence of advanced visual aids. (In the sequel, we shall drop the qualifier "computational" since we believe that geometry that is useful in real life is by nature more or less computational. Furthermore, it is difficult to draw lines delimiting what is computational and what is not. It is known that many computational geometry problems make use of the "less computational" geometric ideas [Preparata and Shamos 1985].)

These preliminary thoughts about such a geometer's workbench owe to Macsyma [Mathlab Group 1983], a very sophisticated computer algebra system to assist researchers in solving mathematical problems. (We think that a Macsyma-like geometry system must be the guiding light in searching for a good geometer's workbench.) A user enters symbolic input to Macsyma which in return yields symbolic (or numeric) output. A great deal of knowledge has been stored into Macsyma's knowledge base. (It is thought that 100 man-years went into the development of the system which comprises about 300000 lines of code.) Thus the user has access to mathematical techniques which she may not even fully understand but can painlessly employ to solve a particular problem. Conjectures can be tested easily and fast with Macsyma. The system is simple to use but not at the expense of being simplistic; several problems may require serious programming in the Macsyma command language and mastering the "insides" of the system. In short, Macsyma gives the user room to study problems from a more intellectual viewpoint, leaving the low-level, uninteresting computational details to the computer. It also offers an extensible programming environment. As a matter of fact, there is already a large amount of specialized Macsyma code in the so-called SHARE libraries.

Doing geometry, like algebra and many other research endeavors, is an iterative process. We define problems, draw figures, pose conjectures, redraw things, revise our ideas, etc. This exploratory process must be equipped with effective aids to graph data, to draw 2- and 3-dimensional figures to convey as much information as possible, to discover properties, and to store all this information in meaningful and easily retrievable format. These tools must not require a large amount of initial training but have to be powerful. Generally, they should only make their functionality apparent to a user, but when required the internals of the system should allow reprogrammability, editability, and so on. These requirements are satisfied in one way or another by Macsyma. The Lisp programming environment that has evolved during the past two decades of artificial intelligence research also delivers these. The recent Lisp machines, for instance, combine the Lisp programming environment with powerful graphics. (Since Macsyma's base language is Lisp, these machines naturally support Macsyma.) The top level of a Lisp system is a read-evaluate-print loop that repeatedly reads expressions from the input stream, evaluates them, and prints their outcomes on the output stream. Basic data structures are recursively-defined linked objects. Flexible structure editors, debuggers, and execution tracers provide a rich environment for *rapid prototyping,* an emerging pragmatical philosophy in software development. Windows enhance the interaction and, menus and the use of a pointing device such as a mouse frees the user from being keyboard-bound.

What kind of geometric know-how would one expect from a workbench built upon such a workstation? First and foremost, it must be possible to perform conceptually trivial operations such as Voronoi partitions, convex hulls, polyhedral boolean operations, and so on without undue emotional trauma. It is known that implementation of even simple geometric algorithms is difficult because of numerical problems and the number of special cases that warrant special care. Franklin [private communication 1985] mentions the case of intersecting two polygons, a seemingly trivial operation which can result in about 1000 lines of Fortran code once all the cases, such as polygons with multiple components that may or may not intersect the other polygon and whose edges may coincide with other edges or vertices, are taken into account.

Algorithm and data structure animation techniques are also found to be of crucial assistance in this respect. Since a personal workstation has a much friendlier user interface, the user may gain an insight by real-time observation of the outputs from algorithms. A classical example for the need for the latter is derived from the weakness of a bare asymptotic analysis of an algorithm. It is not clear how efficient some of the asymptotically optimal e.g. Voronoi and point-location algorithms are when applied to scenes with only say, tens of objects.

Another key requirement for a geometer's workbench is the availability of good update facilities. This refers to the users ability to add new geometric objects and/or to delete the existing ones. It also embodies the concept of modifying (operating on) existing objects to obtain new ones. For instance, one should be able to take a cube, slice it in the corners and drill a hole in its middle to obtain a new object, and give it a name. One must be able to take the convex hull of say, three, polyhedra and create a new polyhedron.

The preceding operations require that the system has a good understanding of what an object is. For example, if a cube has a hole it means that one can have a sufficiently small object pass through that hole; this would be trivial knowledge had the system possess a pair of eyes but in the lack of that it has to be stored in some way along with the cube. Similarly, it is normally an illicit operation to take the convex hull of two polyhedra, since the convex hull operation is normally defined for a set of points. However, the operation makes sense and must be allowed once it is understood that we are in fact dealing with the vertices of the polyhedra under consideration.

The presentation of especially 3-dimensional visual information must be made in a natural manner. The need for real-time flight simulators has motivated work in the visible surface problem with moving objects. Can this work be incorporated to such a workbench? (These simulators run on very fast hardware.) As another exercise in friendly visual interface, consider the following problem: Construct the Voronoi tesselation of the 3-dimensional space by a set of points. The question is: How can one present the output in the most meaningful manner? Color would help, transparency would help, and finally the ability to selectively review a few regions (polyhedra) would help.

We have only touched upon some key problems that a future geometer's workbench has to provide. Only experience in developing prototypes will demonstrate the validity and completeness of our views. However, we believe that the main philosophy will stay the same: a window- and menu-oriented inter-face with powerful visual presentation features, a set of geometric functions similar in scope and generality to the algebraic functions of Macsyma, ability to pursue several common activities in parallel, and algorithm and data structure animation.

5.2. SP - A Program to Compute Shortest Paths

SP consists of a family of programs written in Franz Lisp [Wilensky 1984] and some functions in Macsyma command language [Mathlab Group 1983] to exper-iment with shortest paths in 3-space. (There are also some Fortran parts of SP which implement the graphical output.) The following description is only cursory and the reader is referred to [Akman 1985] for details of the system.

The program was designed with the following philosophy in mind. Let a workspace including a set of polyhedra be given. SP, using the geometric descriptions of the specified polyhedra, computes shortest paths in this workspace. It has some interactive graphics facilities and can supply the user with the views of the workspace so that she can have an intuitive feeling about the correctness of a particular computation. (In geometric computations, visual debugging is very effective.) In this sense, SP resembles to Verrilli's [1984] sys-tem; it provides the user with facilities to carry out the needed computations, once in a while asking for her intervention here and there. Following a rapid prototyping approach we either simply excluded those computations which we do not currently know how to perform effectively, or reformulated them to be controlled by user advice at certain points. Due to its loosely coupled structure, it is easy to upgrade SP with new algorithms when they become available.

Currently, one can work with a single convex polyhedron using the Franz part of SP. There are facilities to solve BOUNDARY FINDPATH, EXTERIOR FINDPATH, and BOUNDARY FINDPATH (locus). It is also possible to imple-ment an approximate FINDPATH algorithm for a workspace with several convex polyhedra, as outlined in section 3.1 (figures 3.1 and 3.2). Using Macsyma parts of SP it is feasible to compute shortest paths in a general workspace although this is not fully automated in the light of the combinatorial explosion that known FINDPATH algorithms have. Nevertheless, if the user specifies the list of edges that the shortest path must touch, then the problem is solvable. There are also facilities based on Macsyma functions to deal with FINDPATH (locus) but this is not automated yet. (All the symbolic computations in [Franklin and Akman

1985] were done in this way.)

Since it was built as a research tool, the prospective user is expected to know the internals of SP. Fortunately, the interactive nature of Lisp comes into play whenever one wants to debug and/or inspect the current computation and data structures. Working with SP is incremental in the sense that one computes things, stops and studies them (by plotting if necessary), and continues. To make a rough analogy, it is useful to visualize SP as a sophisticated calculator tailored uniquely for shortest path computations. We shall now briefly describe the system and give some examples computed by it (also see figures 3.5 and 4.1).

We first summarize how to solve a system of equations with purely algebraic methods in Macsyma. (This is what OPTIMAL LINE VISIT requires.) Macsyma has a built-in function to solve a system of polynomial equations. Since that function is slow and ineffective for more than three or four equations, we also implemented the Newton-Raphson and optimization approaches of section 2.1 to solve OPTIMAL LINE VISIT. They both work extremely well although there is still a problem of guessing a good starting estimate. (Note however that, in an interactive system like SP this poses no problem; once we detect that the computation is diverging, we simply abort it and restart with a new estimate. Normally, a few such tries will get us to the correct answer. Our experience is that this works even in problem instances with up to a dozen lines.)

SP has facilities to read and check the consistency of polyhedral objects. It can also give extensive statistical information about an object. Once a polyhedron is read, SP builds the edge, vertex, and face data structures to access it easily. SP has a facility to compute as many face visit sequences as required in the *Fgraph* of the polyhedron. Another facility unfolds a given face visit sequence onto the *xy*-plane. In such a development all polygons must have *z*-coordinates either 0 or within its ε-neighborhood. SP checks whether this holds true. Figures 5.1 and 5.2 depict some example paths computed from the developments and then mapped back to the surface of the object, in perspective. (SP did not have a truly interactive graphics output; picture files were saved and plotted off-line.)

For EXTERIOR FINDPATH facilities exist to compute visibility relationships and construct the silhouettes. Then a new object is created and the shortest path computation proceeds routinely. Figure 5.3 is an example object created in this way from a cube. For a situation as in figure 3.1, SP has a function to find the intersections of the given polyhedra with the *s*-to-*g* line segment and to return a list of point pairs for each polyhedron intersecting the segment. Once these tuples are available a BOUNDARY FINDPATH is performed for each pair and its associated polyhedron. Further path optimization can also be incorporated. For BOUNDARY FINDPATH (locus), SP uses a naive Voronoi program. Figure 5.4 was generated by this program. Since the system is essentially graphical, we have not seen a need to implement a point-location routine.

We regard SP as a first-order and rather modest approximation to the large and more general workbench we have proposed in the preceding section. The realization of the latter will entail the integration of additional geometric know-how from classical geometry and faster algorithms from computer science. Better ways will be found to animate algorithms and to visualize complex geometric situations. It is envisaged that such a workbench will broaden the way geometry is done in the style Macsyma accomplished for algebra.

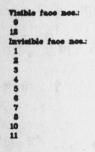

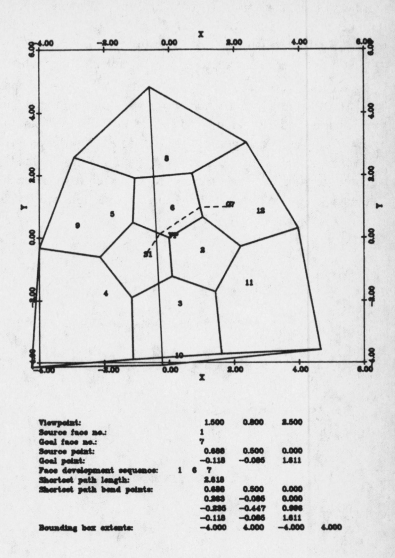

Figure 5.1 Shortest paths on the boundary of a dodecahedron.
Both (a) and (b) are shortest paths. This is a perspective view of
the object as computed by SP.

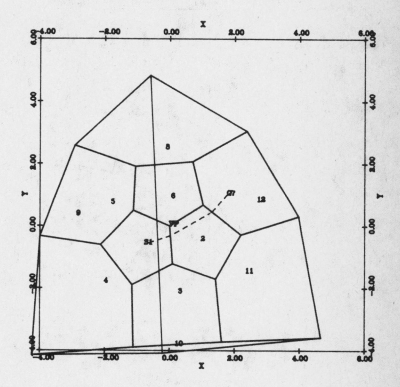

Visible face nos.:
9
12
Invisible face nos.:
1
2
3
4
5
6
7
8
10
11

Viewpoint:		1.500	0.800	2.500	
Source face no.:		1			
Goal face no.:		7			
Source point:		0.688	0.500	0.000	
Goal point:		-0.118	-0.085	1.611	
Face development sequence:	1 2 7				
Shortest path length:		2.613			
Shortest path bend points:		0.688	0.500	0.000	
		0.000	0.276	0.000	
		-0.496	-0.085	0.996	
		-0.118	-0.085	1.611	
Bounding box extents:		-4.000	4.000	-4.000	4.000

(b)

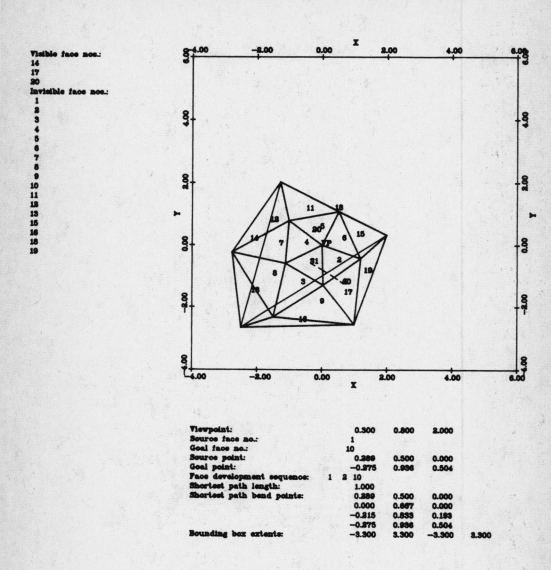

Figure 5.2 A shortest path on the boundary of an icosahedron. This was computed by SP.

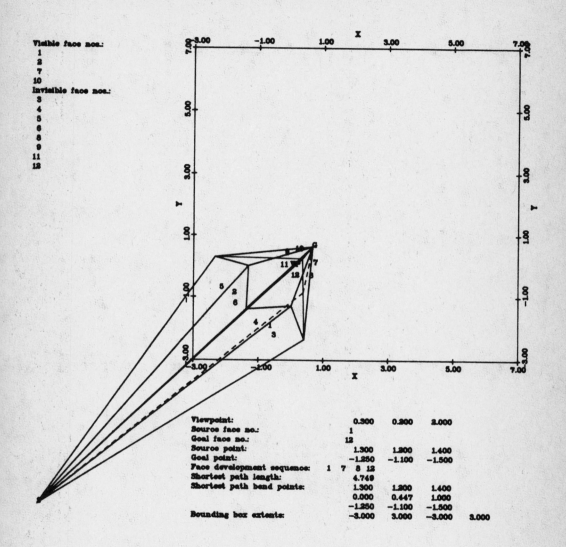

Figure 5.3 A shortest path around a cube. This was computed by
SP after computing the new object and then applying BOUN-
DARY FINDPATH on it.

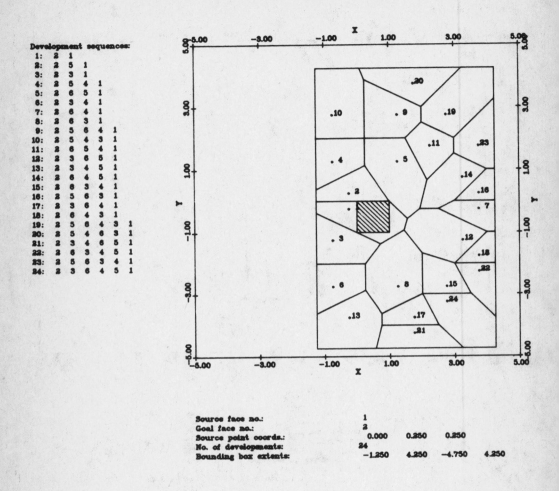

Development sequences:
1: 2 1
2: 2 5 1
3: 2 3 1
4: 2 5 4 1
5: 2 6 5 1
6: 2 3 4 1
7: 2 6 4 1
8: 2 6 3 1
9: 2 5 6 4 1
10: 2 5 4 3 1
11: 2 6 5 4 1
12: 2 3 6 5 1
13: 2 3 4 5 1
14: 2 6 4 5 1
15: 2 6 3 4 1
16: 2 5 6 3 1
17: 2 3 6 4 1
18: 2 6 4 3 1
19: 2 5 6 4 3 1
20: 2 5 4 6 3 1
21: 2 3 4 6 5 1
22: 2 6 3 4 5 1
23: 2 5 6 3 4 1
24: 2 3 6 4 5 1

Source face no.:	1		
Goal face no.:	2		
Source point coords.:	0.000	0.250	0.250
No. of developments:	24		
Bounding box extents:	−1.250	4.250	−4.750	4.250

Figure 5.4 This shows the partitioning of the boundary of a cube
in the presence of a source on face 1. Parts (a), (b), (c), (d), and
(e) respectively show the regions induced on goal faces 2, 3, 4, 5,
and 6. These figures were computed by SP.

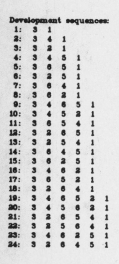

Development sequences:

1:	3	1				
2:	3	4	1			
3:	3	2	1			
4:	3	4	5	1		
5:	3	6	5	1		
6:	3	2	5	1		
7:	3	6	4	1		
8:	3	6	2	1		
9:	3	4	6	5	1	
10:	3	4	5	2	1	
11:	3	6	5	4	1	
12:	3	2	6	5	1	
13:	3	2	5	4	1	
14:	3	6	4	5	1	
15:	3	6	2	5	1	
16:	3	4	6	2	1	
17:	3	6	5	2	1	
18:	3	2	6	4	1	
19:	3	4	6	5	2	1
20:	3	4	5	6	2	1
21:	3	2	6	5	4	1
22:	3	2	5	6	4	1
23:	3	4	6	2	5	1
24:	3	2	6	4	5	1

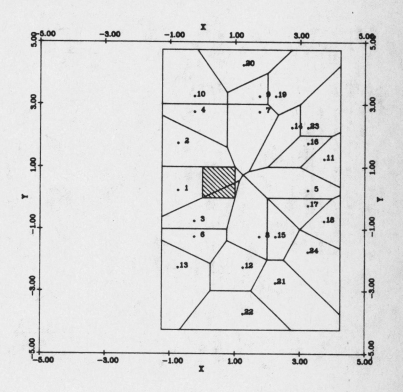

Source face no.:	1			
Goal face no.:	3			
Source point coords.:	0.000	0.250	0.250	
No. of developments:	24			
Bounding box extents:	-1.250	4.250	-4.250	4.750

(b)

Development sequences:
```
 1:  4  1
 2:  4  5  1
 3:  4  3  1
 4:  4  5  2  1
 5:  4  6  5  1
 6:  4  3  2  1
 7:  4  6  3  1
 8:  4  6  2  1
 9:  4  5  6  3  1
10:  4  5  2  3  1
11:  4  6  5  2  1
12:  4  3  6  5  1
13:  4  3  2  5  1
14:  4  6  3  2  1
15:  4  6  2  5  1
16:  4  5  6  2  1
17:  4  3  6  2  1
18:  4  6  2  3  1
19:  4  5  2  6  3  1
20:  4  6  5  2  3  1
21:  4  3  2  6  5  1
22:  4  6  3  2  5  1
23:  4  5  6  2  3  1
24:  4  3  6  2  5  1
```

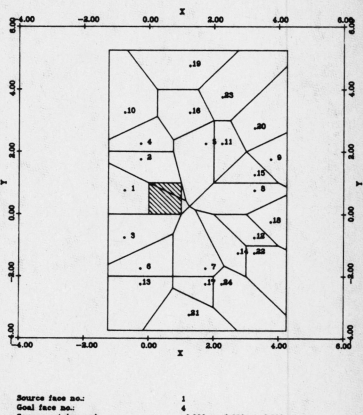

Source face no.:	1		
Goal face no.:	4		
Source point coords.:	0.000	0.250	0.250
No. of developments:	24		
Bounding box extents:	-1.250	4.250	-3.750	5.250

(c)

Development sequences:

1:	5	1				
2:	5	4	1			
3:	5	2	1			
4:	5	4	3	1		
5:	5	6	4	1		
6:	5	2	3	1		
7:	5	6	3	1		
8:	5	6	2	1		
9:	5	4	6	3	1	
10:	5	4	3	2	1	
11:	5	6	4	3	1	
12:	5	2	6	4	1	
13:	5	2	3	4	1	
14:	5	6	3	4	1	
15:	5	6	2	3	1	
16:	5	4	6	2	1	
17:	5	2	6	3	1	
18:	5	6	3	2	1	
19:	5	4	6	3	2	1
20:	5	4	3	6	2	1
21:	5	2	3	6	4	1
22:	5	6	2	3	4	1
23:	5	4	6	2	3	1
24:	5	2	6	3	4	1

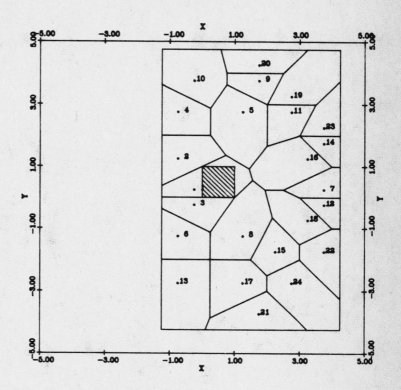

Source face no.:	1			
Goal face no.:	5			
Source point coords.:	0.000	0.250	0.250	
No. of developments:	24			
Bounding box extents:	−1.250	4.250	−4.250	4.750

(d)

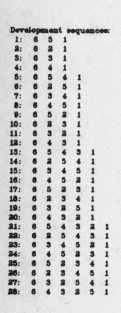

Development sequences:
```
 1:  6  5  1
 2:  6  2  1
 3:  6  3  1
 4:  6  4  1
 5:  6  5  4  1
 6:  6  2  5  1
 7:  6  3  4  1
 8:  6  4  5  1
 9:  6  5  2  1
10:  6  2  3  1
11:  6  3  2  1
12:  6  4  3  1
13:  6  5  4  3  1
14:  6  2  5  4  1
15:  6  3  4  5  1
16:  6  4  5  2  1
17:  6  5  2  3  1
18:  6  2  3  4  1
19:  6  3  2  5  1
20:  6  4  3  2  1
21:  6  5  4  3  2  1
22:  6  2  5  4  3  1
23:  6  3  4  5  2  1
24:  6  4  5  2  3  1
25:  6  5  2  3  4  1
26:  6  2  3  4  5  1
27:  6  3  2  5  4  1
28:  6  4  3  2  5  1
```

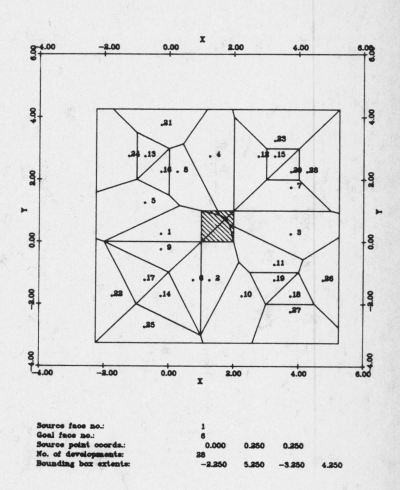

Source face no.:	1			
Goal face no.:	6			
Source point coords.:	0.000	0.250	0.250	
No. of developments:	28			
Bounding box extents:	-2.250	5.250	-3.250	4.250

(e)

6. Conclusion and Future Work

This final chapter has two sections. In section 6.1 we summarize the contributions of this monograph. In section 6.2 we offer directions for future work and cite various research problems.

6.1. Results

The main results of this work can be summarized as follows:

- We have shown that there is an algebraic flavor inherent in FINDPATH. The shortest unobstructed path connecting the source and the goal points possibly bends at some edges of the given obstacles while subtending equal entry and exit angles. The general instance of FINDPATH can then be solved using purely algebraic methods such as elimination. We then have gone on to demonstrate the use of the nonlinear system solvers (of a numeric nature) in solving this problem. In particular, Newton-Raphson and optimization methods were found to be effective in solving OPTIMAL LINE VISIT, a major ingredient of FINDPATH. (Recent implementation work by Bajaj [April 1986] also supports this view strongly.)

- We have given two new algorithms to solve FINDPATH when the source and the goal points are located in a workspace which has a single polyhedron. In the first case (BOUNDARY FINDPATH), the given points are on the polyhedron's surface. In the second case (EXTERIOR FINDPATH), they are outside the polyhedron. These algorithms use planar developments and polyhedral visibility.

- We have described the advantages of Voronoi diagrams in two locus cases for FINDPATH. In one case, there is a single convex polyhedron and only a source point on it is given. We then partition the boundary of this polyhedron so that future queries with new goal points can be answered quickly. In doing so, we make use of standard planar point-location algorithms for a straight-edge planar subdivision, for querying. In the other case, we hint the possibility of a space partitioning scheme to solve the same problem for many polyhedra (albeit very inefficiently for the time being). This partitions the free space around the given polyhedra into regions bounded by high-order surfaces so that the shortest paths for all goals in a given region follow identical sequence of edges of the given polyhedra. Our method makes use of a recent spatial point-location algorithm (which in turn is based on an important tool of algebraic geometry known as cylindrical algebraic decomposition) for arbitrary algebraic varieties.

- We have introduced the idea of a "Geometer's Workbench," a powerful work-station equipped with elaborate software to deal with geometry problems. In addition to introducing a set of desirable functionalities and specifications for such a workbench, we completed the preliminary version of an exemplary system called SP to compute shortest paths. This prototype comprises a family of Lisp and Macsyma programs which implement the algorithms and the techniques mentioned above. SP lets the user to run her programs interactively and renders graphical output. To the best of our knowledge, the shortest path pictures computed by SP are the first ones in 3-space.

6.2. Future Research and Open Problems

We obviously answered only a small section of the problems posed by FINDPATH in this text. There are many interesting problems deserving further study. These are listed below in no particular order. (An asterisk identifies, in our view, an especially difficult problem.)

- *FINDPATH (*):* Is there an algorithm whose execution time is provably polynomial in workspace complexity (e.g. the total number of vertices) to solve FINDPATH? This is an intriguing question and although we believe that the answer is no, a proof would require new developments in complexity theory. Just to remind the reader the fastest growing nature of the field, it is noted that in the first version of this work [Akman 1985], we have posed the following question: Is there an algorithm whose execution time is provably lower than doubly exponential in workspace complexity? (Remember that the doubly exponential bound follows directly from elimination theory.) It is a remarkable result that Reif and Storer [1985], using the technique of Collins [1975], were able to answer this question in the affirmative. Another promising research path to take may be to inquire about the complexity of approximate solutions. An approximate solution to FINDPATH is a path which has length either very close to the optimal (i.e. Papadimitriou's algorithm below), or at most a constant times the optimal (not unlike Christofides' algorithm [Garey and Johnson 1979] which approximates

GEOMETRIC TRAVELING SALESMAN) There is an encouraging result in this area, namely, the fully polynomial approximation scheme of Papadimitriou [1985]. Papadimitriou's result is also interesting in that it is, like Khachiyan's linear programming algorithm, has a term in the complexity bound depending on the size of the longest integer used by the algorithm (cf. section 4.3).

- *OPTIMAL LINE (EDGE) VISIT (*):* We again believe that the answer to this problem becomes intractable when the ordered visit requirement is relaxed. Sufficiently fast numerical methods may be designed to solve the ordered version which also seems to be intractable with purely algebraic methods. We shall have more to say about this problem before closing this chapter.

- *BOUNDARY FINDPATH:* Regarding the shortest paths on a convex polyhedron with n vertices, is $O(n^2\log n)$ a lower (preprocessing) bound [Mitchell et al 1985] for this problem?

- *BOUNDARY FINDPATH (locus):* How does the Voronoi diagram on the boundary of a convex polyhedron change when the source point moves? Theoretically, this would amount to parametrizing the diagram's edge set with respect to the source coordinates so that it can be guessed how they will change metrically while the source moves on the boundary. Note however that the change in the diagram is by no means continuous, i.e. there will be certain "jump" points at which the diagram on a given face of the polyhedron will gain a new topology. Accounting for this effect seems difficult. Franklin [private communication 1985] suggested that one can make movies (say, by animating our algorithm presented in section 4.1 for various sources) showing the effect of different locations of the source, to study this problem experimentally. We find this is an exciting idea especially because it is easily implementable within SP.

- *FINDPATH (locus):* We think that the first thing to do to advance our knowledge about this problem is to build an experimental system. This must be similar to Verrilli's [1984] program in concept, however utilizing more sophisticated data structures and operations. A major problem which does not exist in Verrilli's 2-dimensional system is to find effective ways of communicating the 3-dimensional visual information about surfaces.

- *Algebraic Surfaces (*):* We are particularly interested in finding the intersection (curve) of two arbitrary surfaces efficiently and reliably. The latter requirement necessarily dictates a symbolic (rather than numeric) approach to the problem since there may be all kinds of degeneracies. Another relevant problem is to enumerate the regions of 3-space separated by several surfaces which may intersect each other in all conceivable ways [Arnon et al 1984, parts I and II]. Although there are many useful results on the intersections of algebraic varieties in the area of algebraic geometry, their introduction to the realm of computational geometry has begun only recently [Chazelle 1984].

- *Polyhedra with Higher Genus and Curved Boundary:* Given a boundary description for a polyhedron, one is first required to determine where the holes are. This problem has been completely solved with the well-known classification of 2-manifolds; however we are not aware of any practical program doing this for a given polyhedral description. Also note that, as long as the source and/or the goal is not inside it, a *bounded cavity* (a single-ended hole as in figure 6.1) cannot contribute to the shortest path computation and thus can be "filled." (N.B. The implicit assumption here is that the "entrance" of the cavity is planar. When this is violated the filling must be done with care and only partially.) Curved objects make shortest path computations extremely difficult, e.g. there may be an innumerable number of shortest paths. This is a domain where utilization of the variational calculus techniques may prove useful. Shortest paths on fancy objects such as Möbius bands and Klein bottles are also confusing.

- *FINDPATH for a Single Nonconvex Polyhedron (*):* Efficient algorithms for this problem must not exist in the light of the following informal argument. Assume that we can find shortest paths in the presence of a single nonconvex polyhedron efficiently. We shall show that we can then solve, in a rather strong sense, the general version with many obstacles efficiently too. To see this, imagine that we tie the given polyhedra together with thin "connectors" to obtain one big nonconvex polyhedron. A connector may be considered as a thin prism which runs between two polyhedra while avoiding others (figure 6.2). (This may have interesting connections to "stabbing lines" and finding "transversals" of simple objects as introduced by Edelsbrunner [1985].) Any answer for the big object is an answer for our initial workspace with many obstacles since the probability that a shortest path

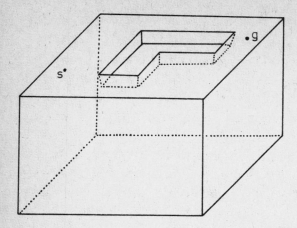

Figure 6.1 A bounded cavity which can be safely filled.

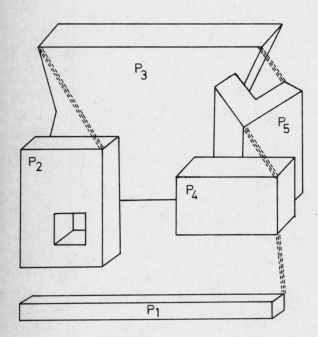

Figure 6.2 A family of connectors in a general workspace
constructing a big polyhedron.

intersects a connector can be made sufficiently small by reducing the connector thickness to a small ε.

- *Good (Rather than Optimal) Paths:* Clearly, no real task-level robot system would like to compute the shortest paths since the latter by definition tend to touch the obstacles [Hopcroft 1986]. On the other hand, finding good paths which avoid the obstacles comfortably is not a well-defined problem (at least in computational geometry) since the meaning of "good" here is necessarily subjective [Nguyen 1984]. For example, if there exists a torus-like obstacle in the workspace, in general one might require that no robot path pass through its hole. In that case, none of the inner paths (no matter how comfortably it avoids the torus) would be good.

- *Monte-Carlo Algorithms:* Monte-Carlo algorithms [Hammersley and Handscomb 1964] constitute a very powerful paradigm in problem solving; yet their value is often underestimated and it is somewhat discouraging to observe that most of the research dealing with Monte-Carlo techniques is not fully appreciated in computer science. (This situation is rapidly changing, cf. [Kirkpatrick et al 1983].) We believe that such methods should be useful in path planning although there is no representative work that we can report here dealing with shortest paths. We hope to make a starting effort with the following approach which is taken from [Rubinstein 1981].

For the following discussion, we shall reconsider the objective function $D(x_1, x_2, \cdots, x_n)$ introduced in section 2.1. The goal of OPTIMAL LINE VISIT is to minimize D, that is:

$$\min_{x \varepsilon U} D(x) = D(\bar{x}) = \bar{D}$$

where U is a subset of the n-dimensional Euclidean space R^n. The following result is important in what follows:

THEOREM 6.1. Let $D(x) = D(x_1, x_2, \cdots, x_n)$ be a real-valued continuous function over a closed bounded domain U of R^n. Further assume there is a unique point $\bar{x} \varepsilon U$ at which $\min_{x \varepsilon U} D(x)$ is attained. (There are no restrictions on relative minima.) Then the coordinates $\bar{x}_i$ of the minimization point are given by:

$$\bar{x}_i = \lim_{\lambda \to \infty} \frac{\int_U x_i e^{-\lambda D(x)} dx}{\int_U e^{-\lambda D(x)} dx}$$

for all i such that $1 \leq i \leq n$.

Proof. This is based on the Laplace formula and is attributed to Pincus [Rubinstein 1981]. □

The Monte-Carlo method that we shall summarize below is known as the *Metropolis procedure* and is based on the pioneering work of Metropolis et al [1953]. (It is interesting to observe that the Metropolis procedure is also at the heart of the so-called "simulated annealing" or "cooling" procedures which solve the NP-complete problems approximately [Kirkpatrick et al 1983].) Since for fixed λ in the above formula one gets the following ratio of integrals:

$$\frac{\int\limits_U x_i e^{-\lambda D(x)} dx}{\int\limits_U e^{-\lambda D(x)} dx}$$

we shall deal with the problem of approximating this ratio. For large λ the major contribution to these integrals come from a small neighborhood of $\bar{x}$, the minimizing point. Metropolis procedure is based on simulating a Markov chain that spends *most* of the time visiting states near the point $\bar{x}$.

Specifically, consider partitioning U to N mutually disjoint regions U_j's and replace the integrals over U by appropriate Riemann sums. (Assume for simplicity that all regions have equal volume.) Take a point $y^j \varepsilon U_j$ and construct an ergodic (irreducible) Markov chain $\{X_k\}$ with state space $\{y^1, y^2, \cdots, y^N\}$ and with transition probabilities p_{ij}, $1 \leq i, j \leq N$, satisfying the condition $\pi_j = \sum\limits_i \pi_i p_{ij}$, $j = 1, \cdots, N$, where $\{\pi_j\}$ is the invariant distribution for the Markov chain. Using the strong law of large numbers for Markov chains, it follows that:

$$m^{-1} \sum_1^m X_k \to \bar{x}$$

as $m \to \infty$, with probability 1. Metropolis constructs the Markov chain with the required invariant distribution as follows. Start with a symmetric transition probability matrix $P^* = (p_{ij}^*)$ where $1 \leq i, j \leq N$, and the known values $\pi_i \pi_j^{-1}$. Define the transition matrix of the Markov chain $\{X_k\}$ as in the following cases:

$p_{ij} = p_{ij}^* \pi_j \pi_i^{-1}$, if $\pi_j \pi_i^{-1} < 1$ where $i \neq j$

$p_{ij} = p_{ij}^*$, if $\pi_j \pi_i^{-1} \geq 1$ where $i \neq j$

and finally,

$$p_{ij} = p_{ii}^* + \sum_{l\,:\,\pi_l < \pi_i} p_{ij}(1 - \pi_l \pi_i^{-1}), \text{ where } i = j$$

Then it is possible to demonstrate that the Markov chain with the above transition matrix has the invariant distribution $\{\pi_i\}$, in other words, $\pi_i = \sum_j p_{ij} \pi_j$.

It is straightforward to realize a chain with such a transition matrix. The details will be omitted here and the reader is referred to [Rubinstein 1981] for a full description of this procedure. In the light of the very optimistic results reported in e.g. [Kirkpatrick et al 1983], there is good reason to believe that Metropolis-like algorithms are probably the ultimate answer to the previously intractable problems of multiextremal optimization.

References

Abelson, H. and A. DiSessa, *Turtle Geometry: The Computer as a Medium for Exploring Mathematics,* MIT Press, Cambridge, MA (1982).

Akman, V. and W.R. Franklin, "On the question 'Is $\sum_{1}^{n}\sqrt{a_i} \leq L$?'," *Bulletin of the EATCS,* (28) pp. 16-20 (February 1986).

Akman, V., *Minimal path problems in model-based robot programming: A literature survey,* Tech. rep. IPL-TR-042, Image Processing Lab, Rensselaer Polytechnic Institute, Troy, N.Y. (January 1983).

Akman, V., *Shortest paths avoiding polyhedral obstacles in 3-dimensional Euclidean space,* PhD dissertation, Electrical, Computer, and Systems Eng. Dept., Rensselaer Polytechnic Institute, Troy, N.Y. (June 1985).

Aleksandrov, A.D., *Konvexe Polyeder,* Akademie-Verlag, Berlin (1958).

Arnon, D.S., G.E. Collins, and S. McCallum, "Cylindrical algebraic decomposition II: An adjacency algorithm for the plane," *SIAM Journal on Computing* **13**(4) pp. 878-889 (November 1984).

Arnon, D.S., G.E. Collins, and S. McCallum, "Cylindrical algebraic decomposition I: The basic algorithm," *SIAM Journal on Computing* **13**(4) pp. 865-877 (November 1984).

Asano, Ta., Te. Asano, L. Guibas, J. Hershberger, and H. Imai, "Visibility of disjoint polygons," *Algorithmica* **1**(1) pp. 49-63 (1986).

Avis, D. and B.K. Bhattacharya, "Algorithms for computing the d-dimensional Voronoi diagrams and their duals," pp. 159-180 in *Advances in Computing Research,* ed. F.P. Preparata, JAI Press (1983).

Avis, D., T. Gum, and G.T. Toussaint, *Visibility between two edges of a simple polygon,* Tech. rep. SOCS-85.20, School of Computer Science, McGill University, Montreal (October 1985).

Bajaj, C., *The algebraic complexity of shortest paths in polyhedral spaces,* Tech. rep. CSD-TR-523, Dept. of Computer Science, Purdue University, West Lafayette, IN (June 1985).

Bajaj, C., "An efficient parallel solution for Euclidean shortest path in three dimensions (preliminary version)," *Proc. IEEE Conf. on Robotics and Automation,* pp. 1897-1900 (April 1986).

Bajaj, C., "Limitations to algorithm solvability: Galois methods and models of computation (preliminary version)," *Proc. ACM Symp. on Symbolic and Algebraic Computation,* (July 1986).

Bajaj, C. and T.T. Moh, *Generalized unfoldings for shortest paths in Euclidean 3-space,* Tech. rep. CSD-TR-526, Dept. of Computer Science, Purdue University, West Lafayette, IN (July 1985).

Bajaj, C., "Proving geometric algorithm non-solvability: An application of factoring polynomials," *Journal of Symbolic Computation* 2(1) pp. 99-102 (March 1986).

Bieri, H. and W. Nef, "A recursive sweep-plane algorithm determining all cells of a finite division of R^d," *Computing* 28(3) pp. 189-198 (1982).

Boyse, J.W., "Interference detection among solids and surfaces," *Communications of the ACM* 21(1) pp. 3-9 (January 1979).

Brooks, R.A. and T. Lozano-Perez, *A subdivision algorithm in configuration space for Findpath with rotation,* AI Memo No. 684, Artificial Intelligence Lab, Massachusetts Institute of Technology, Cambridge, MA (December 1982).

Brooks, R.A., "Solving the Findpath problem by good representation of free space," *IEEE Transactions on Systems, Man, and Cybernetics* 13(3) pp. 190-197 (March 1983).

Canny, J., "Collision detection for moving polyhedra," *IEEE Transactions on Pattern Analysis and Machine Intelligence* 8(2) pp. 200-209 (March 1986).

Cartwright, D. and T.C. Gleason, "The number of paths and cycles in a digraph," *Psychometrika* 31(2) pp. 179-199 (June 1966).

Chazelle, B.M., *Fast searching in a real algebraic manifold with applications to geometric complexity,* Tech. rep. CS-84-13, Dept. of Computer Science, Brown University, Providence, R.I. (June 1984).

Chein, O. and L. Steinberg, "Routing past unions of disjoint linear barriers," *Networks* 13 pp. 389-398 (1983).

Chew, L.P., "Planning the shortest path for a disc in $O(n^2 \log n)$ time," *Proc. 1st ACM Symp. on Computational Geometry*, pp. 214-220 (June 1985).

Collins, G.E., "The calculation of multivariate polynomial resultants," *Journal of the ACM* 18(4) pp. 515-532 (October 1971).

Collins, G.E., "Quantifier elimination for real closed fields by cylindrical algebraic decomposition," *Proc. 2nd GI Conf. on Automata Theory and Formal Languages (Lecture Notes in Computer Science 33)*, pp. 134-183 (1975).

Courant, R. and H. Robbins, *What is Mathematics?*, Oxford University Press, New York (1941).

Dobkin, D.P. and R.J. Lipton, "Multidimensional searching problems," *SIAM Journal on Computing* **5**(2) pp. 181-186 (1976).

Donald, B.R., *Hypothesizing channels through free-space in solving the Findpath problem,* AI Memo No. 736, Artificial Intelligence Lab, Massachusetts Institute of Technology, Cambridge, MA (June 1983).

Donald, B.R., *The Mover's problem in automated structural design,* Lab for Computer Graphics and Spatial Analysis, Graduate School of Design, Harvard University, Cambridge, MA (August 1983).

O'Dunlaing, C., M. Sharir, and C.K. Yap, *Generalized Voronoi diagrams for a ladder: II. Efficient construction of the diagram,* Tech. rep. 140 (Robotics rep. 33), Computer Science Division, Courant Institute of Mathematical Sciences, New York University (November 1984).

O'Dunlaing, C., M. Sharir, and C.K. Yap, *Generalized Voronoi diagrams for moving a ladder: I. Topological analysis,* Tech. rep. 139 (Robotics rep. 32), Computer Science Division, Courant Institute of Mathematical Sciences, New York University (November 1984).

O'Dunlaing, C., M. Sharir, and C.K. Yap, "Retraction: A new approach to motion-planning," *Proc. 15th ACM Symp. on Theory of Computing,* pp. 207-220 (April 1983).

O'Dunlaing, C. and C.K. Yap, "A 'retraction' method for planning the motion of a disc," *Journal of Algorithms* **6** pp. 104-111 (1985).

Eastman, C.M., "Representations for space planning," *Communications of the ACM* **13**(4) pp. 242-250 (April 1970).

Edelsbrunner, H., "Finding transversals of sets of simple geometric figures," *Theoretical Computer Science* **35** pp. 55-69 (1985).

Edelsbrunner, H., L.J. Guibas, and J. Stolfi, "Optimal point location in a monotone subdivision," *SIAM Journal on Computing* **5**(2) pp. 317-340 (May 1986).

Edelsbrunner, H. and H.A. Maurer, "A space-optimal solution of general region location," *Theoretical Computer Science* **16** pp. 329-336 (1981).

Efimov, N.V., "Qualitative problems of the theory of deformation of surfaces," pp. 274-423 in *Differential Geometry and Calculus of Variations,* AMS Translations Series (1962).

Foley, J.D. and A. van Dam, *Fundamentals of Interactive Computer Graphics,* Addison-Wesley, Reading, MA (1982).

Franklin, W.R. and V. Akman, "Euclidean shortest paths in 3-space, Voronoi diagrams with barriers, and related complexity and algebraic issues," pp. 895-917 in *Fundamental Algorithms for Computer Graphics,* ed. R.A. Earnshaw,Springer-Verlag (1985).

Franklin, W.R. and V. Akman, "Locus techniques for shortest path problems in robotics," in *Proc. IFAC Symp. on Robot Control*, Pergamon Press (August 1986).

Franklin, W.R. and V. Akman, "Partitioning the space to calculate shortest paths to any goal around polyhedral obstacles," *Proc. 1st Annual Workshop on Robotics and Expert Systems*, pp. 45-52 (June 1985).

Franklin, W.R. and V. Akman, "Shortest paths between source and goal points located on/around a convex polyhedron," *Proc. 22nd Allerton Conf. on Communication, Control, and Computing*, (September 1984).

Franklin, W.R., V. Akman, and C. Verrilli, "Voronoi diagrams with barriers and on polyhedra for minimal path planning," *The Visual Computer* **1** pp. 133-150 (1985).

Franklin, W.R. and V. Akman, "A workbench to compute unobstructed shortest paths in 3-space," *SIAM Conf. on Geometric Modeling and Robotics*, (July 1985).

Franklin, W.R., *Partitioning the plane to calculate minimal paths to any goal around obstructions*, Electrical, Computer, and Systems Eng. Dept., Rensselaer Polytechnic Institute, Troy, N.Y. (November 1982).

Frechet, M. and K. Fan, *Initiation to Combinatorial Topology*, Prindle-Weber-Schmidt, Boston, MA (1967).

Garcia, C.B. and W.I. Zangwill, "Finding all solutions to polynomial systems and other systems of equations," *Mathematical Programming* **16** pp. 159-176 (1979).

Garcia, C.B. and W.I. Zangwill, *Pathways to Solutions, Fixed Points, and Equilibria*, Prentice-Hall, Englewood Cliffs, N.J. (1981).

Garey, M.R., R.L. Graham, and D.S. Johnson, "Some NP-complete geometric problems," *Proc. 8th Annual ACM Symp. on Theory of Computing*, pp. 10-22 (May 1976).

Garey, M.R. and D.S. Johnson, *Computers and Intractability: A Guide to the Theory of NP-Completeness*, W.H. Freeman, San Francisco, CA (1979).

Goldberg, M., "A solution of problem 66-11: Moving furniture through a hallway," *SIAM Review* **11** pp. 75-78 (1969).

Grunbaum, B., *Convex Polytopes*, John Wiley, New York (1967).

Guibas, L.J. and J. Stolfi, "Primitives for the manipulation of general subdivisions and the computation of Voronoi diagrams," *ACM Transactions on Graphics* **4**(2) pp. 74-123 (April 1985).

Hammersley, J.M. and D.C. Handscomb, *Monte-Carlo Methods*, Chapman and Hall, London (1964).

Harary, F., *Graph Theory*, Addison-Wesley, Reading, MA (October 1972).

Heindel, L.E., "Integer arithmetic algorithms for polynomial real zero determination," *Journal of the ACM* **18**(4) pp. 533-548 (October 1971).

Hildebrant, S. and A. Tromba, *Mathematics and Optimal Form*, Scientific American Books, Inc., New York (1985).

Hopcroft, J.E., "The impact of robotics on computer science," *Communications of the ACM* **29**(6) pp. 486-498 (June 1986).

Hopcroft, J.E., D.A. Joseph, and S.H. Whitesides, *Determining points of a circular region reachable by joints of a robot arm*, Tech. rep. TR-82-516, Computer Science Dept., Cornell University, Ithaca, N.Y. (1982).

Hopcroft, J.E., D.A. Joseph, and S.H. Whitesides, "Movement problems for 2-dimensional linkages," *SIAM Journal on Computing* **13**(3) pp. 610-629 (August 1984).

Hopcroft, J.E., D.A. Joseph, and S.H. Whitesides, "On the movement of a robot arm in 2-dimensional bounded regions," *SIAM Journal on Computing* **14**(2) pp. 315-333 (May 1985).

Hopcroft, J.E., J.T. Schwartz, and M. Sharir, "On the complexity of motion planning for multiple independent objects: PSPACE-hardness of the Warehouseman's problem," *International Journal of Robotics Research* **3**(4) pp. 76-88 (Winter 1984).

Hopcroft, J.E. and G. Wilfong, "Motion of objects in contact," *International Journal of Robotics Research* **4**(4) pp. 32-46 (Winter 1986).

Hopcroft, J.E. and G. Wilfong, *Reducing multiple object motion planning to graph searching*, Tech. rep. TR-84-616, Computer Science Dept., Cornell University, Ithaca, N.Y. (1984).

Howden, W.E., "The Sofa problem," *Computer Journal* **11**(3) pp. 299-301 (November 1968).

Jacobson, R.A. and K.L. Yocom, "Paths of minimal length within a cube," *American Mathematical Monthly* **73** pp. 634-639 (June 1966).

Jacobson, R.A. and K.L. Yocom, "Shortest paths within polygons," *American Mathematical Monthly* **73** pp. 868-872 (October 1966).

Johnson, D.S. and C.H. Papadimitriou, "Computational complexity and the Traveling Salesman problem," in *The Traveling Salesman Problem*, ed. E.L. Lawler, J.K. Lenstra, A.H. Rinooy Kan, D.B. Shmoys,John Wiley, New York (August 1985).

Joseph, D.A. and W.H. Platinga, "On the complexity of reachability and motion planning questions (extended abstract)," *Proc. 1st ACM Symp. on Computational Geometry*, pp. 62-66 (June 1985).

Kantabutra, V. and S.R. Kosaraju, "New algorithms for multilink robot arms," *Journal of Computer and System Sciences* **32**(1) pp. 136-153 (February 1986).

Katoh, N., T. Ibaraki, and H. Mine, "An efficient algorithm for k-shortest simple paths," *Networks* **12** pp. 411-427 (1982).

Kedem, K., R. Livne, J. Pach, and M. Sharir, "On the union of Jordan regions and collision-free translational motion amidst polygonal obstacles," *Discrete and Computational Geometry* **1**(1) pp. 59-71 (1986).

Kedem, K. and M. Sharir, "An efficient algorithm for planning collision-free translational motion of a convex polygonal object in 2-dimensional space amidst polygonal obstacles," *Proc. 1st ACM Symp. on Computational Geometry,* pp. 75-80 (June 1985).

Kirkpatrick, D.G., "Efficient computation of continuous skeletons," *Proc. 20th IEEE Annual Symp. on the Foundations of Computer Science,* pp. 18-27 (October 1979).

Kirkpatrick, S., C.D. Gelatt, Jr., and M.P. Vecchi, "Optimization by simulated annealing," *Science* **220**(4598) pp. 671-680 (13 May 1983).

Kirkpatrick, D.G., "Optimal search in planar subdivisions," *SIAM Journal on Computing* **12**(1) pp. 28-35 (February 1983).

Klee, V., "On the complexity of d-dimensional Voronoi diagrams," *Archiv der Mathematik* **34** pp. 75-80 (1980).

Ku, S.Y. and R.J. Adler, "Computing polynomial resultants: Bezout's determinant vs. Collins' reduced PRS algorithm," *Communications of the ACM* **12**(1) pp. 23-30 (January 1969).

Larson, R.C. and V.O.K. Li, "Finding minimum rectilinear distance paths in the presence of barriers," *Networks* **11**(3) pp. 285-304 (September 1981).

Lazard, D., "Resolution des systemes d'equations algebriques," *Theoretical Computer Science* **15** pp. 77-110 (1981).

Lee, D.T. and R.L. Drysdale, "Generalization of Voronoi diagrams in the plane," *SIAM Journal on Computing* **10**(1) pp. 73-87 (February 1981).

Lee, D.T., "On k-nearest neighbor Voronoi diagrams in the plane," *IEEE Transactions on Computers* **31**(6) pp. 478-487 (June 1982).

Lee, D.T. and F.P. Preparata, "Computational geometry - A survey," *IEEE Transactions on Computers* **33**(12) pp. 1072-1101 (December 1984).

Lee, D.T. and F.P. Preparata, "Euclidean shortest paths in the presence of rectilinear barriers," *Networks* **14** pp. 393-410 (1984).

Lee, D.T. and F.P. Preparata, "Location of a point in a planar subdivision and its applications," *SIAM Journal on Computing* **6**(3) pp. 594-606 (September 1977).

Lee, D.T., *Proximity and reachability in the plane,* PhD dissertation, University of Illinois at Urbana-Champaign (1978).

Leven, D. and M. Sharir, "An efficient and simple motion planning algorithm for a ladder moving in two-dimensional space amidst polygonal barriers (extended abstract)," *Proc. 1st ACM Symp. on Computational Geometry,* pp. 221-227 (June 1985).

Lipski, W. Jr., "Finding a Manhattan path and related problems," *Networks* **13**(3) pp. 399-409 (September 1983).

Lipton, R.J. and R.E. Tarjan, "Applications of a planar separator theorem," *SIAM Journal on Computing* **9**(3) pp. 615-627 (August 1980).

Lipton, R.J. and R.E. Tarjan, "A separator theorem for planar graphs," *SIAM Journal on Applied Mathematics* **36**(2) pp. 177-189 (April 1979).

Lozano-Perez, T., "Automatic planning of manipulator transfer movements," *IEEE Transactions on Systems, Man, and Cybernetics* **11** pp. 681-698 (1981).

Lozano-Perez, T., "Spatial planning: A configuration space approach," *IEEE Transactions on Computers* **32**(2) pp. 108-120 (February 1983).

Lozano-Perez, T. and M.A. Wesley, "An algorithm for planning collision-free paths among polyhedral objects," *Communications of the ACM* **22**(10) pp. 560-570 (October 1979).

Lyusternik, L.A., *Shortest Paths, Variational Problems,* Macmillan, New York (1964).

Maruyama, K., "An approximation method for solving the Sofa problem," *International Journal of Computer and Information Sciences* **2** pp. 29-48 (1973).

Group, Mathlab, *MACSYMA Reference Manual (2 Volumes),* Lab for Computer Science, Massachusetts Institute of Technology, Cambridge, MA (1983).

Mehlorn, K., *Multi-dimensional Searching and Computational Geometry (Data Structures and Algorithms, 3 Volumes),* Springer-Verlag, Heidelberg (1984).

Metropolis, N., A.W. Rosenbluth, M.N. Rosenbluth, A.H. Teller, and E. Teller, "Equation of state calculations by fast computing machines," *Journal of Chemical Physics* **21**(6) pp. 1087-1092 (June 1953).

Mignotte, M., "Identification of algebraic numbers," *Journal of Algorithms* **3** pp. 197-204 (1982).

Mitchell, J.S.B., D.M. Mount, and C.H. Papadimitriou, *The discrete geodesic problem,* Operations Research Dept., Stanford University, Stanford, CA (1985).

Mitchell, J.S.B. and C.H. Papadimitriou, "Planning shortest paths (extended abstract)," *SIAM Conf. on Geometric Modeling and Robotics*, (July 1985).

Mitchell, J.S.B. and C.H. Papadimitriou, *The weighted region problem,* Operations Research Dept. Stanford University, Stanford, CA (1985).

Mitchell, J.S.B., *Shortest rectilinear paths among obstacles,* Operations Research Dept., Stanford University, Stanford, CA (1986).

Moravec, H.P., *Obstacle avoidance and navigation in the real world by a seeing robot rover,* PhD dissertation, Computer Science Dept., Stanford University, Stanford, CA (September 1980).

Morgan, A.P., "A method of computing all solutions to systems of polynomial equations," *ACM Transactions on Mathematical Software* **9**(1) pp. 1-17 (March 1983).

Moser, L., "Problem 66-11: Moving furniture through a hallway," *SIAM Review* **8** p. 381 (1966).

Moses, J., "Solution of systems of polynomial equations by elimination," *Communications of the ACM* **9**(8) pp. 634-637 (August 1966).

Mount, D.M., "Storing the subdivision of a polyhedral surface," *Proc. 2nd ACM Symp. on Computational Geometry,* (June 1986).

Nguyen, V-D., *The Findpath problem in the plane,* AI Memo No. 760, Artificial Intelligence Lab, Massachusetts Institute of Technology, Cambridge, MA (February 1984).

Overmars, M.H., *The locus approach,* Tech. rep. RUU-CS-83-12, Vakgroep Informatica, Rijksuniversiteit Utrecht (July 1983).

Papadimitriou, C.H., "An algorithm for shortest-path motion in three dimensions," *Information Processing Letters* **20**(5) pp. 259-263 (June 1985).

Papadimitriou, C.H., "The Euclidean Traveling Salesman problem is NP-complete," *Theoretical Computer Science,* pp. 237-244 (1977).

Preparata, F.P., "A new approach to planar point location," *SIAM Journal on Computing* **10**(3) pp. 473-482 (August 1981).

Preparata, F.P. and S.J. Hong, "Convex hulls of finite sets of points in two and three dimensions," *Communications of the ACM* **20**(2) pp. 87-93 (February 1977).

Preparata, F.P. and M.I. Shamos, *Computational Geometry: An Introduction,* Springer-Verlag, New York (1985).

Provan, J.S., *The complexity of reliability computations in planar and acyclic graphs,* Tech. rep. 83/12, Operations Research and Systems Analysis Curriculum, University of North Carolina at Chapel Hill (December 1984).

Reif, J.H., "Complexity of the Mover's problem and generalizations (extended abstract)," *Proc. 20th Annual IEEE Symp. on Foundations of Computer Science*, pp. 421-427 (October 1979).

Reif, J.H. and M. Sharir, "Motion planning in the presence of moving obstacles," *Proc. 26th Annual IEEE Symp. on the Foundations of Computer Science*, pp. 144-154 (1985).

Reif, J.H. and J.A. Storer, *Shortest paths in Euclidean space with polyhedral obstacles*, Tech. rep. CS-85-121, Computer Science Dept., Brandeis University, Waltham, MA (April 1985).

Rezende, P.J. de, D.T. Lee, and Y.F. Wu, "Rectilinear shortest paths with rectangular barriers," *Proc. 1st ACM Symp. on Computational Geometry*, pp. 204-213 (June 1985).

Richards, I., "An application of Galois theory to elementary arithmetic," *Advances in Mathematics* **13** pp. 268-273 (1974).

Rohnert, H., *New algorithms for shortest paths avoiding convex polygonal obstacles*, Tech. rep. A86/02, Fachbereich Angewandte Mathematik und Informatik, Universitat des Saarlandes, Saarbrucken (1986).

Rohnert, H., *Shortest paths in the plane with convex polygonal obstacles*, Tech. rep. A85/06, Fachbereich Angewandte Mathematik und Informatik, Universitat des Saarlandes, Saarbrucken (1985).

O'Rourke, J., S. Suri, and H. Booth, "Shortest paths on polyhedral surfaces," *Proc. 2nd Annual Symp. on Theoretical Aspects of Computer Science (Lecture Notes on Computer Science 182)*, pp. 243-254 Springer-Verlag, (January 1985).

Rowat, P.F., *Representing spatial experience and solving spatial problems in a robot environment*, PhD dissertation, University of British Columbia, Vancouver (1979).

Rubinstein, R.Y., *Simulation and the Monte-Carlo Method*, John Wiley & Sons, Inc., New York (1981).

Saaty, T., *Optimization in Integers and Related Extremal Problems*, McGraw-Hill, New York (1970).

Schwartz, J.T. and M. Sharir, "On the Piano Mover's problem: I. The case of a two-dimensional rigid polygonal body moving amidst polygonal barriers," *Communications on Pure and Applied Mathematics* **36** pp. 345-398 (1983).

Schwartz, J.T. and M. Sharir, "On the Piano Mover's problem: V. The case of a rod moving in three-dimensional space amidst polygonal obstacles," *Communications on Pure and Applied Mathematics* **37** pp. 815-848 (1984).

Schwartz, J.T. and M. Sharir, "On the Piano Mover's problem: II. General techniques for computing topological properties of real algebraic manifolds," *Advances in Applied Mathematics* **4** pp. 298-351 (1983).

Schwartz, J.T. and M. Sharir, "On the Piano Mover's problem: III. Coordinating the motion of several bodies: The special case of circular bodies moving amidst polygonal barriers," *International Journal of Robotics Research* **2**(3) pp. 46-75 (Fall 1983).

Sebastian, J., "A solution to problem 66-11: Moving furniture through a hallway," *SIAM Review* **12** pp. 582-586 (1970).

Sedgewick, R., *Algorithms*, Addison-Wesley, Reading, MA (1983).

Shamos, M.I., *Computational geometry*, Ph.D. dissertation, Dept. of Computer Science, Yale University, New Haven, CT (1978).

Shamos, M.I. and D. Hoey, "Closest-point problems," *Proc. 16th IEEE Annual Symp. on the Foundations of Computer Science*, pp. 151-162 (October 1975).

Sharir, M. and E. Ariel-Sheffi, "On the Piano Mover's problem: IV. Various decomposable two-dimensional motion planning problems," *Communications on Pure and Applied Mathematics* **37** pp. 479-493 (1984).

Sharir, M. and A. Schorr , "On shortest paths in polyhedral spaces," *SIAM Journal on Computing* **15**(1) pp. 193-215 (February 1986).

Spirakis, P. and C.K. Yap, "Strong NP-hardness of moving many discs," *Information Processing Letters* **19**(1) pp. 55-59 (26 July 1984).

Sussman, G.J., *A Computer Model of Skill Acquisition*, American Elsevier, New York (1975).

Sutherland, I.E., R.F. Sproull, and R.A. Schumacker, "A characterization of ten hidden-surface algorithms," *ACM Computing Surveys* **6**(1) pp. 1-55 (March 1974).

Tarjan, R.E., *Data Structures and Network Algorithms*, CBMS-NSF Regional Conf. Series in Applied Mathematics, SIAM Publications, Philadelphia, PA (1983).

Tarski, A., *A Decision Method for Elementary Algebra and Geometry*, University of California Press (1951).

Tompa, M., "An optimal solution to a wire-routing problem," *Journal of Computer and System Sciences* **23** pp. 127-150 (1981).

Toussaint, G.T., *Shortest path solves edge-to-edge visibility in a polygon*, Tech. rep. SOCS-85.19, School of Computer Science, McGill University, Montreal (September 1985).

Udupa, S., *Collision detection and avoidance in computer-controlled manipulators,* PhD dissertation, Electrical Eng. Dept., California Institute of Technology, Pasadena, CA (1977).

Valiant, L.G., "The complexity of enumeration and reliability problems," *SIAM Journal on Computing* **8**(3) pp. 410-421 (August 1979).

Waerden, B.L. van der, *Algebra (2 Volumes),* Frederick Ungar, New York (1977).

Verrilli, C., *One-source Voronoi diagrams with barriers: A computer implementation,* MS thesis, Electrical, Computer, and Systems Eng. Dept., Rensselaer Polytechnic Institute, Troy, N.Y. (February 1984).

Wangdahl, G.E., S.M. Pollock, and J.B. Woodward, "Minimum-trajectory pipe routing," *Journal of Ship Research* **18** pp. 46-49 (1974).

Welzl, E., "Constructing the visibility graph for n line segments in $O(n^2)$ time," *Information Processing Letters* **20**(4) pp. 167-171 (May 1985).

Wilensky, R., *LISPcraft,* W.W. Norton & Company, New York (1984).

Winston, P.H., *Artificial Intelligence,* Addison-Wesley, Reading, MA (1977).

Wong, T., *Minimum rectangular distance paths between two points on a plane with barriers,* BS thesis, Electrical Eng. and Computer Science Dept., Massachusetts Institute of Technology, Cambridge, MA (May 1979).

Yen, J.Y., "Finding the k-shortest loopless paths in a network," *Management Science* **17**(11) pp. 712-716 (July 1971).